#TIL
TODAY I LEARNED

#TIL

TODAY I LEARNED

Hilarious, Entertaining, and Educational Trivia

BY STEPHEN SPIGNESI

Skyhorse Publishing

Skyhorse Publishing books may be purchased in bulk at special discounts for sales promotion, corporate gifts, fund-raising, or educational purposes. Special editions can also be created to specifications. For details, contact the Special Sales Department, Skyhorse Publishing, 307 West 36th Street, 11th Floor, New York, NY 10018 or info@skyhorsepublishing.com.

Skyhorse® and Skyhorse Publishing® are registered trademarks of Skyhorse Publishing, Inc.®, a Delaware corporation.

Visit our website at www.skyhorsepublishing.com.

10 9 8 7 6 5 4 3 2 1

Library of Congress Cataloging-in-Publication Data is available on file.

Cover design by Kai Texel
Cover illustration by Getty Images

Print ISBN: 978-1-5107-5551-2
Ebook ISBN: 978-1-5107-5552-9

Printed in the United States of America

#TIL
TODAY I LEARNED

This is for Rachel Montgomery,
uno dei miei più cari amici.

Pal, you got skills.

Ancora imparo.
I am still learning.

Michelangelo

L'apprendimento non esaurisce mai la mente.
Learning never exhausts the mind.

Leonardo da Vinci

10 OBSERVATIONS ABOUT LEARNING

1.

*"Anyone who stops learning is old,
whether at twenty or eighty."*
Henry Ford

2.

*"Learning is not attained by chance, it must be sought
for with ardor and attended to with diligence."*
Abigail Adams

3.

*"Tell me and I forget. Teach me and I remember.
Involve me and I learn."*
Benjamin Franklin

4.
"Live as if you were to die tomorrow.
Learn as if you were to live forever."
Mahatma Gandhi

5.
"Leadership and learning are
indispensable to each other."
John F. Kennedy

6.
"He who learns but does not think, is lost!
He who thinks but does not learn is in great danger!"
Confucius

7.
"A man only learns in two ways. One, by reading,
and the other by association with smarter people."
Will Rogers

8.
"Seeing much, suffering much, and studying much,
are the three pillars of learning."
Benjamin Disraeli

9.

"I like to listen. I have learned a great deal from listening carefully. Most people never listen."
Ernest Hemingway

10.

"You're always learning. The problem is, sometimes you stop and think you understand the world. This is not correct. The world is always moving. You never reach the point you can stop making an effort."
Paulo Coelho

INTRODUCTION
A MATTER OF FACT

We hope this book provides exactly what the subtitle says: facts and trivia that are funny, entertaining, and educational.

I've been a full-time writer since the mid-eighties, but I also spent a decade teaching composition and literature to first year college students. In the end, they taught *me*. They taught me how to provide information that they would enjoy learning, and ultimately remember and use in their education and their lives.

This was not, and *is* not an easy task. Attention spans today are *short*. In fact, they're *really* short. If you don't capture the reader, listener, watcher almost immediately, they will, my friend, *move on*.

Be sincere; be brief; be seated.
Franklin D. Roosevelt

The longest entry in this book is just over 150 words. The briefest, a single sentence of a fewer than a dozen words.

Our plan? You find the entries in this tome funny, entertaining, and educational . . . as well as the perfect antidote for a short attention span. So, onward, and may the facts be with you!

Stephen Spignesi
New Haven, CT
September 2, 2019

500 #TIL FACTOIDS

#TIL 1. American writer Stephen King was almost killed on June 20, 1999 when a Maine man named Bryan Smith struck him with his van as King was walking alongside a Maine road. King was reading a book while walking (*The Store* by Bentley Little), something he was known to do. King needed multiple surgeries and full recovery took years. Since Stephen King is a writer known for horror novels, some people were not surprised when it was learned that Bryan Smith died in 2000 of a Fentanyl drug overdose on September 21. Why? September 21, 2000 was Stephen King's 53rd birthday.

#TIL 2. The word "CLUB" in Club Sandwich sandwich does not stand for "chicken lettuce under bacon." It's called a Club Sandwich because it was first served in a club.

#TIL 3. The Paris Catacombs, which date from 1774, hold the bones of more than six million people and are a popular tourist attraction, even though the walls are lined with skulls.

#TIL 4. Emily Dickinson wrote close to 1,800 meticulously constructed, lyrical, thematically-specific poems, often using slant rhyme and unconventional grammatical and punctuational elements, while suffering from headaches, iritis, nausea, blackouts, anxiety disorder, severe hypertension, heart failure, bipolar disorder, possible depression, and possible agoraphobia.

#TIL 5. Russia censored the 2019 Elton John movie *Rocketman* before allowing it to be shown in the country. They edited out a gay sex scene and the end text scene which reported that Elton was happily married to David Furnish and that they were raising two sons. Elton spoke out against the censoring.

#TIL 6. America has already had a gay president: James Buchanan, our fifteenth president. Buchanan had a twenty-three-year friendship with the only never-married vice president William Rufus King. (King was VP under Franklin Pierce.) Buchanan and King were referred to by the media as "Miss Nancy and Aunt Fancy." In a letter to a confidante dated May 13, 1844, Buchanan wrote about his life after King moved to Paris to become the American ambassador to France: "I am now 'solitary and alone,' having no companion in the house with me. *I have gone a wooing to several gentlemen, but* *have not succeeded with any one of them."* Sounds gay to us. Not that there's anything wrong with that.

#TIL 7. *Downton Abbey* is one of the most popular and successful British historical dramas ever created. One of the most beloved characters in the show is Violet Crawley, the Dowager Countess of Grantham, played by the inestimable Maggie Smith. During a 2015 interview on *The Graham Norton Show*, Maggie Smith admitted that, even though she has the boxed set, she has never watched the series.

#TIL 8. In 1888, the New York State Commission on Capital Punishment issued a report on various methods of execution that the state could actually put into practice. The study had been helmed by Elbridge T. Gerry, grandson of founding father Elbridge Gerry. Methods they studied included tying the victim to the mouth of a cannon and then firing the cannon, burning alive, burying alive, crucifixion, and dichotomy, which consisted of sawing someone in half, while they're alive and conscious, of course. None of the methods were ever put into use.

#TIL 9. Thousands of 8-legged mites live on our faces. They eat your dead skin cells and lay eggs on the rim of your follicles and pores. They save up their poop until they die, and then they explode all over your skin.

#TIL 10. As part of a possibly apocryphal account of an animal psi experiment, a woman and her pet boxer were each placed in copper-lined rooms, out of sight and earshot of each other. The dog's heart was monitored by electrocardiogram. A male unknown to the woman then suddenly entered the room where she sat, shouted at her, and threatened her with violence. The woman's pet's heart began to race wildly at the precise moment that her mistress was in danger. The dog was alone in the room at the time and could not hear or see anything that was going on in the other room.

#TIL 11.   On Tuesday, June 4, 2019, a swarm of ladybugs a mile above San Diego was so large it showed up on the National Weather Service's radar.

#TIL 12.   Timothy Olyphant was one of the cast members of Quentin Tarantino's 2019 film *Once Upon a Time . . . in Hollywood* who confirmed that Quentin had a hard and fast rule for his movies. Bringing a cellphone onto the set was grounds for immediate firing.

#TIL 13.   In a 2002 study by the University of Hertfordshire and the British Association for the Advancement of Science, 2 million people from 70 countries were asked to vote on the "funniness" of 40,000 jokes. The results revealed that this is the funniest joke of all time:

> *A couple of New Jersey hunters are out in the woods when one of them falls to the ground. He doesn't seem to be breathing and his eyes have rolled back in his head. The other guy whips out his cellphone and calls 911. He gasps to the operator: "My friend is dead! What can I do?" The operator, in a soothing voice, says: "Just take it easy. I can help. First, let's make sure he's dead." There is a silence, then a shot is heard. The guy's voice comes back on the line. He says: "OK, now what?"*

#TIL 14. In 2019, the owners of Ark Encounter, a 510-foot model based on the biblical Noah's Ark, sued its insurers for refusing to cover rain damage.

#TIL 15. Holocaust executioner and medical experimenter Josef Mengele was a collector. He particularly liked to amass large quantities of aborted fetuses, testicles, and surgically removed gallstones. In Robert Jay Lifton's superb study, *The Nazi Doctors*, an anthropological prisoner assistant of Mengele's named Teresa W. tells the story of a simple box and a simple errand. Asked by Mengele to carry a box to another part of the camp, she felt an impulse to open it and see what was inside, only to discover "that it contained glass jars, in which were human eyes."

#TIL 16.   In 1947, Pitney-Bowes ran a print ad for its postage meters with the headline "Is it always illegal to kill a woman?"

#TIL 17.   In a memoir written by Dali's physician Dr. Ben Kean called *M.D.*, Kean revealed that he once requested a price from Dali to paint a portrait of a woman he knew. Dali told him that if he agreed to paint the portrait, no matter what the woman looked like, the painting would be of a fish. Kean respectfully declined the offer.

#TIL 18. In June 2019, a restaurant in Connecticut had to close when fluids from a decomposing body in the apartment upstairs began leaking into the restaurant.

#TIL 19. In January 2019, at the New England Aquarium in Boston, a 30-pound, 10-foot long Anaconda snake named Anna gave birth to eighteen baby snakes, each about two feet long. Anna had never been with a male snake and the other snakes in the exhibit were confirmed females. These were "virgin births" through a process called parthenogenesis, which is reproduction without a male. Anna cloned herself and created eighteen babies. Fifteen of them were stillborn and of the remaining three, two survived. Turns out sharks can do this, too, but it is an exceedingly rare occurrence.

#TIL 20. By 2013, it was estimated that 32.3 quadrillion bullets had already been fired in the videogame *Call of Duty*. That's 32,300,000,000,000,000 digital bullets.

#TIL 21. The first ever attack on a U.S. President took place on Friday, January 30, 1835 when a deranged man named Richard Lawrence fired two guns point blank at President Andrew Jackson. Both guns misfired, so Lawrence was arrested and tried. The prosecutor was Francis Scott Key, composer of "The Star-Spangled Banner." Lawrence ended up in a mental institution for twenty-six years, ultimately dying there.

#TIL 22. Americans drink 400 million cups of coffee a day, every day, which is 146 billion cups per year. America leads the world in coffee consumption, and imports $4 billion worth of coffee each year. Two-thirds of the coffee consumed is during breakfast. Half of all coffee drinkers, if they had to choose between giving up their morning shower or their morning coffee, would give up the shower.

#TIL 23. President Zachary Taylor did not learn of his June 1848 nomination as the Whig candidate for the presidency until a month later because the letter informing him of this decision arrived at his home with ten cents postage due and he wouldn't pay it.

#TIL 24. Ringo Starr's personal copy of the *White Album* (officially released as *The Beatles*) sold at auction in December 2015 for $790,000, making it the most expensive Beatles album ever sold. It was No. 0000001 and proceeds went to the Lotus Foundation, a charitable organization founded by Ringo and his wife Barbara Bach to fund, support, participate in, and promote charitable projects aimed at advancing social welfare in diverse areas, including but not limited to substance abuse, cerebral palsy, brain tumors, cancer, battered women and their children, homelessness, and animals in need. Ringo had kept it in a vault for 35 years.

#TIL 25. It's estimated that there are approximately 32 million atheists in America—10 percent of the population—although that number could be skewed low, since a great many people have admitted when polled that they were ashamed to admit to people that they didn't believe in God.

#TIL 26. According to a 2015 poll conducted for *Parade* magazine, the Top 10 favorite ethnic foods in America are, in order, Chinese, Mexican, Italian, Japanese/Sushi, Greek, French, Thai, Spanish, Indian, and Mediterranean.

#TIL 27. Harriet Beecher Stowe received $10,000 in royalties from sales of *Uncle Tom's Cabin* within six months of the book's publication in 1852. The *London Times* wrote that they believed that that was "the largest sum of money ever received by any author, either American or European, from the sales of a single work in so short a period of time."

#TIL 28. The Peruvian Triangle Weaver Spider uses its web as a slingshot to hurl itself at prey or an enemy.

#TIL 29. In 2019, there were over 1.6 billion websites on the Internet. It is estimated that approximately 75 percent of these sites are inactive. The most popular porn website, Pornhub.com, registered 33.5 billion visits to the site in 2018, an average of 92 million visits per day. (The most popular search term that year on Pornhub was "lesbian.") In comparison, approximately 1.5 billion people log on to Facebook every day.

#TIL 30. Studies have shown that the average person touches their face 2,000 to 3,000 times a day.

#TIL 31. When *Titanic* set sail, she carried enough food and beverages to feed 2,200 people three times a day. (*Titanic*'s capacity was 3,300 passengers and crew, but the ship wasn't full on its maiden voyage.) *Titanic*'s "cupboard" included 40 tons of potatoes, 38 tons of meat, 20,000 bottles of beer, 40,000 eggs and tons more of anything a passenger could possibly desire. It is estimated that all of it was gone within twenty-eight years after her sinking, either from decomposition, or consumption by sea creatures.

#TIL 32. In 1974, Midol ran a print ad that read, "Your guy: Your No. 1 Reason for Midol."

#TIL 33. It's borderline impossible to know with certainty what song is the most covered song of all time, but the Beatles' "Yesterday" is certainly in either the number 1 or number 2 spot. Runners-up include "(I Can't Get No) Satisfaction" by the Rolling Stones, "Imagine" by John Lennon, "White Christmas" by Bing Crosby, "Over the Rainbow" by Judy Garland, and "Cry Me a River" by Julie London.

#TIL 34. By the time he was thirty, George Washington had had smallpox, pleurisy, dysentery, and malaria.

#TIL 35. President Theodore "Teddy" Roosevelt carried a bottle of morphine with him for most of his life. He carried it to self-administer if he ever ended up fatally ill, with an incapacitating disease, away from home. He would choose to end his life rather than endure intractable pain.

#TIL 36. Kim Peek was the real-life inspiration for the "Rain Man" played by Dustin Hoffman in the movie of the same name. Among other talents, Kim could read two pages of a book in three seconds. His left eye read the left page, his right eye read the right page. And he perfectly remembered everything he read.

#TIL 37. In 1975, Rosalyn Carter became the first First Lady to be photographed with a serial killer. Carter posed for a picture with John Wayne Gacy, who was active in Democratic politics at the time. She later signed the photo, "To John Gacy. Best wishes. Rosalynn Carter."

#TIL 38. Speaking of John Wayne Gacy, his last meal before his execution by lethal injection was 12 deep fried shrimp, a bucket of Original Recipe chicken from KFC, a pound of fresh strawberries, french fries, and a Diet Coke.

#TIL 39. Edward Mordrake, a possibly apocryphal heir to English nobility, purportedly had an extra face on the back of his head. The face could smile and sneer, but not eat, talk, or see. Mordrake supposedly committed suicide in the late 1800's at the age of twenty-three, but it is possible that Mordrake never existed and was, in fact, a fictional creation of writer Charles Lotin Hildreth. Although there are accounts of Mordrake in books and medical writings, all reports seem to be drawn from the same inconclusive original sources, and no contemporaneous accounts of his existence exist. There are, however, pictures of Mordrake on the Internet. (Of course there are.)

- -

#TIL 40. In 2019, the top 10 most popular pets in America were, in descending order: dogs, cats, hamsters, fish, mice, guinea pigs, birds, snakes, iguanas, and ferrets.

- -

#TIL 41. There are 14 punctuation marks in English grammar. They are the period [.], question mark [?], exclamation point [!], comma [,], semicolon [;], colon [:], dash [—], hyphen [-], parentheses [( )], brackets [[ ]], braces [{ }], apostrophe ['], quotation marks [" "], and ellipsis [. . .].

#TIL 42. Abraham Lincoln was an official inventor. He received U.S. Patent No. 6469 in May 1849 for a device that would lift boats over shoals. His invention was never built and put into use.

#TIL 43. The smallpox pandemic was the deadliest in world history. It's estimated that between 5,000 BC and 1980 more than 6 billion people died from the disease. Smallpox was officially declared eradicated in 1980. Second runner-up is measles, with a total of 200 million deaths in the last 150 years, and then the Black Death, with approximately 100 million deaths worldwide from 1331 through 1820.

#TIL 44. As of 2019, 1.1 billion people in the world smoke tobacco.

#TIL 45. Thomas Jefferson rewrote the New
Testament. His version was known both as
The Jefferson Bible and *The Life and Morals
of Jesus of Nazareth* and was not published
until seventy-five years after his death. In his
revisions, he removed all of what would be
considered the "paranormal/supernatural"
stuff. No resurrection, virgin birth, walking on
water, changing water into wine, raising the
dead, etc. In his version, Jesus was merely a
man.

#TIL 46. The first doctor to attend to JFK after he was
shot had delivered Lee Harvey Oswald's
daughter Audrey a month earlier.

#TIL 47. Edgar Allan Poe had what they called during
his time a "nervous condition," which we
would likely diagnose today as clinical
depression. As did (and do) so many other
haunted artists, Poe turned to drink in an
attempt to keep at bay the demons who

visited him during his blackest moods. Rather than calm and anesthetize him, though, alcohol turned him into a surly, often raging maniac. He died in 1849 after a 5-day drinking binge. Sounding like one his own characters, his last tortured words were "Lord help my poor soul."

#TIL 48. James Cameron's *Avatar* is the most successful movie of all time with lifetime earnings of $2.79 billion.

#TIL 49. Anesthesia, called the most important invention of the past 2,000 years, brought about the end of surgical pain. Ether was first used in 1841 by Dr. Crawford Long, of Georgia. In 1845, Dr. Horace Wells demonstrated the use of ether during surgery for Harvard Medical School students and a year later, Wells was credited with the discovery/invention of using ether as an anesthetic.

#TIL 50. One of George Washington's sets of false teeth was made of eight human teeth taken from dead soldiers and attached to a piece of carved hippopotamus ivory with solid gold rivets.

#TIL 51. The Beatles' "Hey Jude" and Queen's "Bohemian Rhapsody" were recorded using the same piano.

#TIL 52. Even though graduating from school is the *end* of an academic endeavor, graduation is called "commencement," which means "beginning," because the student is beginning a new phase of his or her life.

#TIL 53. There are approximately 4,200 religions in the world.

#TIL 54. In 1917, the United States Navy ran an ad showing a winsome girl dressed in a Navy uniform saying "Gee!! I wish I were a man. I'd join the Navy." The tagline at the bottom of the ad read, "Be a man and do it." The idea for this ad came from an actual event at a Navy Recruiting Station when a twenty-year-old woman named Bernice Smith walked in and said, "Gee, I wish I were a man, I'd join the Navy." Later that year, Bernice became the first woman to successfully enlist in the Navy as a woman.

#TIL 55. Being knighted is probably the highest honor English monarchy can bestow on a person. Most people accept knighthood proudly. Some people, however, for a variety of reasons, have refused their MBE (Member of the Most Excellent Order of the British Empire), including David Bowie, Vanessa Redgrave, Aldous Huxley, and Doris Lessing. Beatle John Lennon accepted his knighthood but later returned it. He sent it back with a note: "Your Majesty, I am returning this in protest against Britain's involvement in the

Nigeria-Biafra thing, against our support of America in Vietnam and against Cold Turkey slipping down the charts. With Love, John Lennon of Bag."

#TIL 56. Humans are born with around 300 bones. As adults, we have 206. The difference is because dozens of individual bones fuse together throughout childhood as we age.

#TIL 57. In October 2008, Ringo Starr released a video message to his fans telling them that he would no longer be signing autographs and to please stop sending him stuff to sign. He said, this ban was "in direct response to an inordinate amount of items which have recently appeared for sale on e-bay, and to those that repeatedly send cards and items to be signed."

#TIL 58. According to WalletHub.com, the most pet-friendly city in America is Scottsdale,

Arizona. They used several criteria to arrive at a winner including the number of vets and pet-friendly restaurants in the city, as well as the cost of owning a pet. Orlando, Florida, and Tampa, Florida were numbers two and three, respectively.

#TIL 59. The Sun makes up 99 percent of the Solar System.

#TIL 60. The Eagles are the backing vocalists for Elton John on Elton's song "White Lady White Powder" on his *21 at 33* album.

#TIL 61. Jonah Falcon claims to have the world's largest penis. It measures 13.5 inches erect and Falcon claims to have been sought out for sex by both men and women, including Oscar nominees and winners.

#TIL 62. The songs "A Whiter Shade of Pale" by Procol Harum and "Bohemian Rhapsody" by Queen—the two most played songs on British radio in 2009—both contain the word "fandango."

#TIL 63. According to Google, 129,864,880 books have been published in modern history.

#TIL 64. *Saved from the Titanic* was the first *Titanic* movie, and it's also the only one starring a survivor of the catastrophe. The movie starred Dorothy Gibson, who made the 10-minute silent film almost immediately after her rescue. It debuted on May 14, 1912, only 29 days after the *Titanic* sank. In the movie, Gibson wore the same dress that she wore on the *Titanic*.

#TIL 65. James Henry Pullen (1835–1916) was a savant and a gifted wood sculptor. Pullen was developmentally disabled, mute (although he could say—badly—"mother"), and socially aggressive and antagonistic. He ultimately found his gift of working with wood and went on to sculpt incredible works, including ships and even a guillotine he rigged over the door of a man he disliked. (It misfired.) He was known as the Genius of Earlswood Asylum, which was actually the Royal Earlswood Hospital, known formerly as The Asylum for Idiots and The Royal Earlswood Institution for Mental Defectives, in Redhill, Surrey, England.

#TIL 66. In 2016, deaths by cardiovascular diseases around the world comprised 31.8 percent of all deaths. Deaths by terrorism comprised 0.06 percent.

#TIL 67. U.S. President Theodore "Teddy" Roosevelt once gave a speech after being shot. When the bullet was fired, it struck the folded, fifty-page copy of the speech he had in his jacket pocket. The bullet still entered Roosevelt's body, but the papers had slowed it enough so that it didn't kill him and the damage it did wasn't severe enough to stop him from talking.

#TIL 68. Newborn babies can't cry tears. They just yowl a lot. Their tear ducts haven't formed yet.

#TIL 69. George Harrison co-wrote the Cream song "Badge" as a thank you to Eric Clapton for his performance on "While My Guitar Gently Weeps" on the Beatles' *White Album*. Due to contractual nonsense, George had to be credited as "L'Angelo Misterioso." Initially, the song was credited solely to Clapton, but later to "Clapton/Harrison." And reportedly, Ringo gave them the line about the swans in the park but he was not given any songwriting credit.

#TIL 70. William Hitler, Adolf Hitler's nephew, served in the U.S. Navy during World War II. He once wrote an article titled, "Why I Hate My Uncle . . ."

#TIL 71. Even though Franklin Pierce was the first US president to have a fulltime bodyguard, he was still attacked when he was in office. In 1854, a deranged man threw a hard-boiled egg at him. When caught, the eggsassin (sorry) tried to kill himself with a pocketknife. Pierce didn't press charges.

#TIL 72. The first message sent by telegraph was "What hath God wrought!" and it was sent by inventor Samuel F.B. Morse on May 24, 1844.

#TIL 73. Actor Johnny Depp collects limited edition Barbie dolls and Jack Kerouac memorabilia.

#TIL 74. The New York City subway system carries 1.8 billion passengers a year. This doesn't even come close to the world's busiest metro system, which is in Beijing, which carries 3.4 billion passengers a year.

#TIL 75. Science fiction author Gene Wolfe invented the machine that cooks Pringles.

#TIL 76. Steven Tyler of Aerosmith, on an episode of *The Late Late Show with James Corden*, said he had spent approximately $2 million on drugs during his career as a rock star. He said, "I'm snorting half of Peru," and assured Corden he was serious. Corden declared Tyler his "best guest ever."

#TIL 77. President William McKinley was reportedly Frank Baum's inspiration and model for the character of the Wizard of Oz.

#TIL 78. "Hollow Earthers" believe that the planet Earth is a hollow sphere, and that the interior of the earth is honeycombed with chambers, tunnels, and roads, and has its own atmosphere, ecosystem, and vegetation. Some Hollow Earthers also believe that the inside of the planet is populated by beings that may be responsible for all the UFO sightings on Earth.

#TIL 79. Americans wanted to avoid using the German-sounding name "hamburger" during World War II, so they called burgers "Liberty Steaks." In 2003, Americans employed a similar tactic by referring to french fries as "Freedom Fries" because of France's opposition to the US going to war in Iraq. And french toast became "Freedom Toast."

#TIL 80. The longest filibuster in U.S. Senate history was delivered by Strom Thurmond on behalf of the Civil Rights Act of 1957. It lasted 24 hours and 18 minutes.

#TIL 81.   William Howard Taft was the biggest U.S. president of all time. He stood six feet, two inches tall and weighed in at 332 pounds at his peak. One of his favorite self-deprecating jokes was, "I got off a streetcar and gave my seat to three ladies."

#TIL 82.   There are approximately 100 million acts of sexual intercourse around the world each day.

#TIL 83.   No one was burned at the stake during the Salem witch trials. Twenty people were executed for witchcraft offenses. Nineteen people were hung—15 women and 4 men—and one man was pressed to death. Four convicted women were pardoned, one convicted woman escaped, and one convicted woman died in prison.

#TIL 84. Three billion pizzas are sold in America every year. Americans eat 350 slices of pizza a second.

#TIL 85. Benjamin Franklin invented the catheter to treat his own bladder stones.

#TIL 86. Walter Diemer invented bubble gum while working for the Fleer Chewing Gum Company. The company claimed the copyright and Diemer never saw a dime in royalties from his invention. He reportedly didn't care because he was so happy to have created something that so many people enjoyed.

#TIL 87. Paper money carries more germs than a household toilet and can carry a live virus for 17 days.

#TIL 88. President Harry Truman got his famous "The Buck Stops Here" slogan from a prison. During a visit to the El Reno Federal Reformatory in Oklahoma, Truman saw the sign over the warden's desk and immediately adopted its message as his own. An identical sign was made by the prisoners for President Truman and sent to him on October 2, 1945. It is now on display at the Truman Library, where it has been since 1957.

#TIL 89. The original title of Jane Austen's *Pride and Prejudice* was *First Impressions*.

#TIL 90. The Shroud of Turin is a woven linen cloth 14 feet, 3 inches long and 3 feet, 7 inches wide, with front and rear images of a man on it that many believe is Jesus Christ. Believers say that the Shroud is the actual burial cloth of Jesus Christ and that his image was miraculously "burned" onto the cloth by an explosion of divine energy at the moment of

His resurrection. Skeptics believes that the Shroud is a medieval painting, circa 1260-1390.

#TIL 91. During World War II, American soldiers were given a ration of 22 sheets of toilet paper per day. British soldiers were given 3 sheets per day.

#TIL 92. *Don Quixote* by Miguel de Cervantes is believed to be the best-selling novel of all time, with estimated sales of 500 million copies. *A Tale of Two Cities* by Charles Dickens follows with 200 million copies sold. *The Lord of the Rings* by J.R.R. Tolkien is in third place with an estimated 150 million copies sold. *The Bible* is believed to be the best-selling book of all time with more than 5 billion copies sold.

#TIL 93. According to the BBC, it rains diamonds on Jupiter and Saturn. "[L]ightning storms turn

methane into soot (carbon) which as it falls
hardens into chunks of graphite and then
diamond."

#TIL 94. The difference between knowledge and
wisdom: It's knowledge to know that
tomatoes are the most popular fruit in the
world. It's wisdom to know not to put them in
a fruit salad.

#TIL 95. The U.S. government reported in 2016 that
$62 million in pennies are lost every year
in circulation. That's 6 billion, 200 million
pennies (6,200,000,000). People save them,
lose them, or throw them away.

#TIL 96. The King of Hearts is the only king in a card
deck who does not have a mustache.

#TIL 97. As of June 2016, the song "Happy Birthday
To You" was declared officially in the public
domain. The purported copyright holder,

Warner/Chappelle, had been making $2 million a year licensing public, TV, and movie performances of the song when, in fact, the song had been in the public domain for decades. Warner/Chappelle settled by paying $14 million to people who had licensed use of the song.

#TIL 98. The Honor Walk is when hospital employees, friends, and relatives line the halls of a hospital as the gurney carrying a person who agreed to donate their organs upon their death passes by.

#TIL 99. The original draft of Franklin Delano Roosevelt's Pearl Harbor speech had "a day that will live in world history." FDR crossed out "world history" and wrote in "infamy."

#TIL 100. In the United States, there is one birth every 8 seconds, one death every 12 seconds, 1 migrant entering the country every 33 seconds, making for a net gain of 1 new person every 14 seconds.

#TIL 101. According to the Population Reference Bureau (prb.org), 106 billion people have been born and lived on earth since 50,000 BC. With a current population of approximately 7.7 billion people, this means that the world's current population is 6 percent of all the people who have ever lived.

#TIL 102. O.J. Simpson's white Ford Bronco is currently on display at the Alcatraz East Crime Museum in Pigeon Forge, Tennessee. The car has been described by its owner Mike Gilbert as the second most famous car in U.S. history after the limo in which J.F.K. was shot.

#TIL 103. In a 2019 interview with *Rolling Stone*, Willie Nelson said that smoking marijuana saved his life and helped him live to 85. He said, "I wouldn't be alive. It saved my life, really, I wouldn't have lived 85 years if I'd have kept drinking and smoking like I was when I was 30, 40-years-old. I think that weed kept me from wanting to kill people. And probably kept a lot of people from wanting to kill me, too—out there drunk, running around."

#TIL 104. Woodrow Wilson's wife Edith Bolling Wilson was a descendant of Pocahontas.

#TIL 105. In April 2019, scientists announced the discovery of the fossil of a previously-unknown crab, which they named *Callichimaera perplexa*, which means "perplexing beautiful chimera." The reason they were perplexed is because this crab was one of the weirdest creatures ever. It was about the size of a quarter and had sexually dimorphic limbs, first and second antennae, foot-like mouthparts, and large compound eyes bearing facets and optical lobes. It is believed to have lived between 90 and 95 million years ago.

#TIL 106.   Genghis Khan had over 500 wives.

#TIL 107.   The six cast members of the TV series *Friends*—Courtney Cox, Jennifer Aniston, David Schwimmer, Matt LeBlanc, Matthew Perry, Lisa Kudrow—each receive $20 million a year in royalties for their work on the show.

#TIL 108.   Elton John has played "Your Song" in concert more than any of his other songs. By 2019, the number of times he played it topped 2,000 performances. "Rocket Man (I Think It's Going to Be a Long Long Time)" and "Bennie and the Jets" were numbers 2 and 3 in terms of times played.

#TIL 109.   In 1775, George Washington and his entire household were inoculated against smallpox, thanks to a suggestion by one of Cotton Mather's slaves. He explained that in Africa they would poke a sharp stick into the center of a smallpox pustule on someone with the disease and then stick the point of the stick into the arms of other natives who were not yet infected. After hearing of this clever practice, Washington had it done to himself and his entire household.

#TIL 110. More than 400 million M&M's are manufactured every day.

#TIL 111. At the Auschwitz concentration camp, 3,000 babies were delivered by a Catholic Polish midwife, Stanisława Leszczyńska, during World War II. Only 500 of the babies survived. She is an official candidate for canonization by the Catholic Church.

#TIL 112. It takes 5 quarts of milk to make 1 pound of cheese.

#TIL 113. Atlantis was a legendary island in the Atlantic Ocean west of Gibraltar, said by Plato to have existed circa 9,000 B.C. and to have sunk beneath the sea during an earthquake. Believers say that Atlantis was real and that its inhabitants were superior beings from whom mankind received all of its advanced, technical knowledge, as well as its languages and religions. Skeptics say that Atlantis is a myth created by Plato as part of a Socratic dialogue to illustrate what would happen when a society degenerated into decadence (Atlantis), as compared to a society that espoused fairness, respect, and dignity (Athens).

#TIL 114. Actor John Costelloe, who played Vito Spatafore's boyfriend Jim "Johnny Cakes" Witowski on *The Sopranos,* was a real-life New York City firefighter. He died in 2008 of a self-inflicted gunshot wound.

#TIL 115. In the late 1800s, the vibrator was invented so woman could treat their own symptoms of "female hysteria" at home without having to go to the doctor's office to have their clitoris manually stimulated.

#TIL 116. "The Boneyard" in Arizona consists of 2,600 acres of dry desert soil that the government uses for storage of out of service, decommissioned aircraft. There are currently around 4,000 aircraft at the Boneyard. They are stripped of engines, weaponry, and engine parts when they arrive and the government reaps $550 million a year from selling parts from these aircraft.

#TIL 117. In high school, George W. Bush was a head cheerleader.

#TIL 118. The 1.4 billion people in China each go through three or so pairs of chopsticks a month, for a total usage of 45 billion pairs a year.

#TIL 119. There are more people in California than in Canada.

#TIL 120. Robin Williams' favorite joke involved men wearing tight pants and people being able to tell "what religion you are": *"I found it very difficult being in tights. You're wearing tights and you're doing Shakespeare and they can tell what religion you are."* He told it many times in various forms throughout his career, mainly during interviews and during talk show appearances.

#TIL 121. You can't sneeze in your sleep. The nerves that trigger sneezing are sleeping, too.

#TIL 122. Facebook adds 8 people per second to its membership rolls.

#TIL 123. There are 500,000 Facebook "likes" every minute.

#TIL 124. Facebook generates $33.6 million a day in ad revenue.

#TIL 125. As of 2018, 49 nations in the world had a military dictatorship, single-party dictatorship, monarchy, personalist dictatorship, hybrid dictatorship, or an authoritarian regime ruling the nation.

#TIL 126. A favored dish in Japan is Beetle Grubs. They are marinated and then boiled or fried.

#TIL 127. President Jimmy Carter saw a UFO on January 6, 1969. He said it was huge and changed colors. He reported it to the International UFO Bureau in Oklahoma and filled out the sighting form. Carter's original report is available online.

#TIL 128. In 1936, the American Tobacco Company marketed their Lucky Strike cigarettes with an ad featuring Santa Claus smoking and recommending Luckies.

#TIL 129. U.S. President Calvin Coolidge was taciturn. One of his well-known traits was being a man of few words. There is a classic story about Coolidge that takes place at a party: He was approached by the hostess, who said, "You must talk to me, Mr. President. I made a bet today that I could get more than two words out of you." Coolidge replied, "You lose."

#TIL 130. The Lost Colony of Roanoke was a group of English settlers who disappeared from Roanoke Island, North Carolina, without a trace, sometime between 1587 and 1590, leaving behind nothing but the word "CROATOAN" carved into a fence post. It is likely that the settlers probably traveled to the nearby settlement of Croatoan (on Hatteras Island) and intermingled with the Chesapeake natives there, resulting, a generation later, in Indians who looked like white people and had grey eyes and light-colored hair.

#TIL 131. There are 55 million potholes in America. (And 4,000 holes in Blackburn, Lancashire.)

#TIL 132. Kirlian photography is the process of photographing an object by exposing film in a dark room to ultraviolet light that results from electronic and ionic interactions caused by an electric field. The photograph shows a light, glowing band surrounding the outline of the object. Supporters of Kirlian photography being some kind of supernatural event say that it reveals the supernatural, etheric auras— the "life energy" or "life force"—of both living and, paradoxically, inanimate things. Kirlian photographs are glimpses at the bioenergy in our bodies. Skeptics say that there is nothing whatsoever supernatural or paranormal about the images produced through Kirlian photography. All the photographs show is a corona discharge, fully understandable and explainable, and due to an electrical charge interacting with the moisture in an object.

#TIL 133. Intersex people are born with both male and female sex organs.

#TIL 134. The Presidential Succession Act of 1947 states that the Speaker of the House is next in line to the presidency after the Vice President. This means that in 2019, if Donald Trump and Mike Pence resigned from office, the next President of the United States would be Nancy Pelosi.

#TIL 135. American poet Walt Whitman did not believe that William Shakespeare wrote the plays attributed to him. He didn't believe that someone who had had as little education as

Shakespeare could write such extraordinary works.

#TIL 136. The female human vagina is set at a 130 degree angle.

#TIL 137. In 2002, a Japanese scientist named Professor Susumu Tachi developed a coat which appears to make the wearer invisible. The illusion was demonstrated at Tokyo University as part of an optical camouflage presentation. Professor Tachi's goal is to make camouflaged objects virtually transparent.

#TIL 138. There are 42 buildings in New York City that have their own zip code.

#TIL 139. So far, Franklin Delano Roosevelt, who served twice as long as any other president, has been the only United States president who did not lose a single staff member or member of his administration due to a scandal or an indictment.

#TIL 140. The Sea Wasp Jellyfish has enough venom in it to kill 60 human beings.

#TIL 141. In America, 1.5 million animals are euthanized each year at animal shelters. This is approximately 20-25 percent of the 6-8 million animals handled by shelters each year.

#TIL 142. Ivy League fully nude "posture photos" were taken of all incoming freshmen at Ivy League and Seven Sisters colleges from 1940 through 1960. Photos were taken of incoming freshmen, as well as then-college students Hillary Rodham Clinton, Diane Sawyer, George Bush, and thousands of others. The nude posture photo practice was stopped in the late 1960s and all the pictures were shredded and burned.

#TIL 143. The three most photographed places in the world are Central Park in New York City, Big Ben in London, England, and the Eiffel Tower in Paris France.

#TIL 144. Before he became the 20th president, James A. Garfield wrote a proof of the Pythagorean Theorem that was published in the *New England Journal of Education* and is still discussed in mathematics textbooks today. Rather than using squares to prove the theorem, Garfield's proof uses trapezoids.

#TIL 145. One of the most difficult piano pieces ever composed is "La Campanella" by Franz Liszt and Niccolò Paganini. It features right hand jumps between intervals larger than one octave, sometimes even stretching for two whole octaves within the time of a sixteenth note.

#TIL 146. One of Stephen Hawking's wheelchairs sold at auction for $393,000.

#TIL 147. During dinner one evening at the White House during eighth president Martin Van Buren's administration, a waiter bent over and whispered to Van Buren that the kitchen was on fire. Van Buren calmly excused himself, and went to put out the fire by organizing a bucket brigade. Reportedly, that was the only time Van Buren had ever set foot in the White House kitchen.

#TIL 148. Martin Scorsese loves the Rolling Stones' song "Gimme Shelter." He has used it (so far) in *Goodfellas*, *Casino*, and *The Departed*.

#TIL 149. Nutritionist Chelsey Amir has concluded that a slice of pizza is a better choice for breakfast than most cereals. Why? Because cereal is loaded with sugar and will result in a sugar crash before noon. However, "pizza packs a much larger protein punch, which will keep you full and boost satiety throughout the morning," Amir said.

#TIL 150. Americans eat 20 pounds of rice every year. People in Asia eat 300 pounds a year, and people in the United Arab Emirates eat 450 pounds a year.

#TIL 151. Wild Bill Hickock was shot and killed by Jack McCall while playing poker on August 2, 1876. He fell off the chair, still holding his hand of cards, supposedly consisting of a pair of black aces, a pair of black eights, and the red Jack of Hearts (or Diamonds, or Queen of Diamonds, depending on the source). This hand—aces and eights—soon became known as the Deadman's hand, although many historians now claim that the story of the cards was a fabrication of later chroniclers of the Wild Bill legend and that there is no contemporary evidence of what hand Hickok was holding when he was shot. The only confirmed account of the cards came from Ellis Pierce, a local barber and witness to the shooting. In a letter to Frank J. Wilstach, Pierce wrote, "Bill's hand read 'aces and eights'—two pair, and since that day aces and eights have been known as 'the Deadman's hand' in the Western country."

#TIL 152. Russia has eleven time zones.

#TIL 153. Fecal transplants are 90 percent effective at treating C. diff—Clostridium difficile—an infection that wipes out the healthy bacteria in a person's digestive tract. Implanting someone else's healthy feces repopulates the gut and cures the infection in 9 out of 10 cases.

#TIL 154. The tallest mountain in the entire Solar System is on Mars. It's 13 miles high and has a diameter of 373 miles.

#TIL 155.   Mama Cass of The Mamas and the Papas, whose real name was Eileen and who had an IQ of 165, once owed the IRS $10,000 in back taxes and penalties. According to movie producer Julia Phillips, Mama Cass paid her bill with a truckload of pennies (a million of them) and was cited for contempt by the U.S. government.

#TIL 156.   Frequent masturbation reduces the likelihood of men developing prostate cancer. What's "frequent?" According to WebMD.com, at least twenty-one times a month. Also, a 2013 study conducted by scientist Anthony Santella and senior lecturer Spring Chenoa Cooper at the University of Sydney concluded that masturbation can reduce the risk of Type 2 diabetes.

#TIL 157.   Dutch painter Johannes Vermeer became extremely popular after the publication of the novel *Girl With a Pearl Earring* and the release of the movie of the same name. Art buffs looking to immerse themselves in scads of the master's art were, however, out of luck. There are only 36 authentic Vermeer paintings in existence.

#TIL 158. Oprah Winfrey and Uma Thurman each have size 11 feet.

#TIL 159. The homeless man who John Lennon fed in the 1988 documentary *Imagine* was Curt Claudio. He became fixated on John Lennon's songs and believed they had been written about him. When Claudio offered "You're gonna carry that weight" as an example of a lyric that was about him personally, John corrected him and told him that that line had been written by Paul. Curt Claudio's older brother Ernie Claudio, in a May 19, 2019 post on meetthebeatlesforreal. com, confirmed that Curt died in an ultralight plane crash in California in 1981.

#TIL 160. NASA—the National Aeronautics and Space Administration—was created by President Dwight Eisenhower in 1958. NASA was launched because the Soviet Union had launched *Sputnik 1*, the first artificial satellite in 1957.

#TIL 161. Nasal hairs can continue to move up to 20 hours after death.

#TIL 162. "Brain freeze" from ice cream or any other frigid substance is caused by the blood vessels in the head dilating when the cold substance touches the roof of your mouth.

#TIL 163. According to the Society of Classical Poets, William Shakespeare's "Sonnet 18" is the greatest poem ever written. It begins, "Shall I compare thee to a summer's day?" Number 2 on their list is John Donne's "Holy Sonnet 10" which begins, "Death, be not proud . . ." Number 3 is William Wordsworth's "Daffodils" which begins "I wandered lonely as a cloud . . ."

#TIL 164. A medieval Muslim ophthalmologist named Ali ibn Isa al-Kahhal advised migraine sufferers to tie a dead mole to their head for relief.

#TIL 165. The Ancient Astronaut theory posits that extraterrestrials visited earth sometime between 10,000 and 40,000 years ago, bred with humans, taught prehistoric humans primitive forms of art and science, and built monuments and invented devices that are still extant today. The chief proponent of the Ancient Astronauts Theory is Erich von Däniken, whose 1969 book *Chariots of the Gods* became an international bestseller. Evidence of aliens' presence can be found in seemingly unexplainable artifacts like a 2,000-year-old battery, as well as ancient monuments and archaeological sites such as Easter Island, Stonehenge, and the Nazca lines. All creation myths speak of Gods coming to earth in chariots of fire. According to Von Däniken, these ancient writers were describing the landings of extraterrestrials.

#TIL 166. The Stationmaster at the Kishi train station in southeastern Japan is a 6-year-old Calico cat named Nitama.

#TIL 167. The Sami people live in the northern tips of Scandinavia and Russia. Their language is multifaceted. They even have a word—*busat*—for a bull with one large testicle.

#TIL 168. Country Time Lemonade will reimburse kids who are fined for running lemonade stands.

#TIL 169. Lizzie Borden was the main suspect in the 1892 murder of her father and stepmother. Her cultural and historical reputation notwithstanding, Borden was acquitted.

#TIL 170. According to the American Library Association, there are 116,867 libraries in America. There are 9,057 public libraries, 3,094 academic libraries, 98,460 school libraries, 5,150 special libraries (law, religious, medical, etc.), 239 Armed Forces libraries, and 867 government libraries.

#TIL 171. Cheese is rarely used in Asian food and the reason is that 90 percent of people of East Asian descent are lactose intolerant.

#TIL 172. The continents move continuously at a rate of about 8/10ths of an inch per year.

#TIL 173. Most TV spinoffs are not successful. However a few that succeeded were *Frasier*, a spinoff of *Cheers*, *Star Trek: The Next Generation*, a spinoff of *Star Trek*, *The Jeffersons*, a spinoff of *All in the Family*, and *Better Call Saul*, a spinoff of *Breaking Bad*.

#TIL 174.   A prostitute could make a year's salary at the ancient Greek Olympics.

#TIL 175.   Heroin was invented in Germany in 1894. It was touted as a non-addictive substitute for morphine and sold over the counter for a variety of ailments, including pain, diarrhea, and nervousness. It quickly became very popular.

#TIL 176.   According to the American Society of Plastic Surgeons, there were 1,356 butt lift procedures in the United States in the year 2000. There were 4,767 in 2015, an increase of 252 percent.

#TIL 177.   According to a survey conducted by *Empire Magazine*, the most popular cinematic character of all time is Indiana Jones. James Bond is second, Han Solo, third, Batman is fourth, and *Alien*'s Ellen Ripley comes in at number five.

#TIL 178. The city with the longest name in the world, with 168 letters, is in Thailand. It's called *Krungthepmahanakhon Amonrattanakosin Mahintharayutthaya Mahadilokphop Noppharatratchathaniburirom Udomratchaniwetmahasathan Amonphimanawatansathit Sakkathattiyawitsanukamprasit.* The official English name for the city is Bangkok.

#TIL 179. Michelangelo was a poet as well as a painter and sculptor. He once wrote a poem about how much he hated painting the ceiling of the Sistine Chapel that began, "I've already grown a goiter from this torture, hunched up here like a cat in Lombardy (or anywhere else where the stagnant water's poison) . . ."

#TIL 180.   Today, 65 percent of Americans shower every day.

#TIL 181.   When asked why his signature on the Declaration of Independence was so large, John Hancock joked that it was so King George would be able to read it without his glasses. (That may be an apocryphal story.) Historians today feel, however, that the oversized signature was a deliberate "statement" on his part, so to speak, of the incredibly high regard in which he held himself.

#TIL 182.   The longest English word has 189,819 letters and would run twenty pages in 12 point type on standard 8 ½ x 11 paper. It is the word for a protein known as titin.

#TIL 183.   *The Catcher in the Rye* author J.D. Salinger reportedly (according to his own daughter) drank his own urine and was into Scientology, Buddhism, Hinduism, Christian Science, and acupuncture. On Salinger's orders, his literary agent would burn the author's fan mail.

#TIL 184. The symbol "#" is called an octothorpe, not "hashtag" or "pound." The "octo" refers to the number of points—eight— in its construction.

#TIL 185. The most common cause of death in the U.S. is cardiac problems. The second is cancer. The third, however, is not a disease of any kind: it's accidents, including medical errors.

#TIL 186. Thomas Paine ended up in prison, sentenced to be guillotined for speaking out against the monarchy. This was considered treason and punishable by death. While in prison, he wrote the first part of *The Age of Reason.* He escaped death by a weird coincidence in which the white cross that was supposed to be painted on the cell doors of those who were to die the following day was placed in the wrong place and overlooked by the guards while collecting the doomed.

#TIL 187. The highest-cholesterol food known to man is cooked pork brains, which tops out at 723 milligrams of cholesterol per ounce.

#TIL 188. A deceased Pope has to be buried completely intact, according to the Catholic Church. This means that no Pontiff can be an organ donor.

#TIL 189. The name of the zipper was created by the B.F. Goodrich company in 1923 when they started using the fastener in their rubber boots. They wanted something catchy or their promotional material, so they created a name based on the sound the clasp made when it was opened and closed: *Zip*!

#TIL 190. Benjamin Franklin discovered that pouring oil overboard around the base of a ship when at sea steadied the vessel. This technique was used by Captain Rostron in 1912 to settle the steamship *Carpathia* after it picked up survivors from the *Titanic* sinking.

#TIL 191. The human brain can process one billion billion (1 exaFLOP) calculations per second. Supercomputers can't even come close to that speed.

#TIL 192. A near-death experience (NDE) is the experience of one's soul or consciousness leaving the body at the point of death. Upon being resuscitated, many NDE percipients report common elements, like rushing through a tunnel towards a light, meeting one's dead relatives and others, sensing the love and joy of God, and being told the deceased was not ready to leave earthly existence. Believers say that an NDE is evidence of life after death. It is proof that the consciousness survives death. During an NDE, the soul separates from the body and begins the transition to a higher plane of existence. For some reason, the soul returns to the body, but the experiences the person remembers were real and are what all human beings will go through when they die. Skeptics say that a near-death experience is an hallucinatory event triggered by changes in the neurochemistry of the dying brain. Science can explain all of the commonalities of an NDE as manifestations of the effects of cardiac arrest and other often-fatal conditions.

#TIL 193. When recording his part of Aladdin for the movie of the same name, Robin Williams improvised sixteen hours of material. Williams's will stipulates that none of the outtakes can be used in any *Aladdin* project for twenty-five years after his death, which will be the year 2039.

#TIL 194. According to biblical literalists, Noah's
Ark is the enormous ship built by Noah
on which he carried his family and all the
species of the world during the Great Flood
described in Genesis. Noah built the Ark on
instructions from God, who had decided to
destroy all living things on Earth because of
man's evil ways. Since Noah and his family
lived virtuous lives, God selected them to
survive the flood, repopulate the Earth, and
restore the saved animal species to the wild.
Nonbelievers say that the story of Noah's
Ark is nothing but a biblical myth, which is
quite similar to other worldwide flood myths,
especially the Babylonian story of Gilgamesh.
There may have been a widespread flood at
some point in our prehistory, but the biblical
account of Noah and his ark is a fabricated
exaggeration for fabling purposes.

#TIL 195. At one point, it was believed that there was a
planet between Mercury and the Sun. It was

known as the Planet Vulcan. Albert Einstein disproved the theory, confirming that the calculations that proved the existence of Vulcan were wrong.

#TIL 196. In June 2019, Joy Harjo, a member of the Muskogee Creek Nation, became the United States' first Native American Poet Laureate.

#TIL 197. The Atlas beetle, some of which are the size of a human palm, can move objects 850 times its weight. This would be comparable to a 150-pound human being able to push an object weighing more than 60 tons.

#TIL 198. Benjamin Rush was the only signer of the Declaration of Independence who had a medical degree. In 1786, Benjamin Rush opened a free hospital for the poor and indigent in Philadelphia. This hospital was the first of its kind in America.

#TIL 199. Vincent van Gogh made 2,000 drawings, paintings, watercolors, and sketches in the short period of ten years from 1880 to 1890. In the two months before his death in 1890 from a self-inflicted gunshot wound, he was making two paintings a day. It has long been believed that van Gogh only sold one painting during his life, and that all his success was posthumous. That may not be true. He sold at least two, as well as some drawings. *Tragic, Ironic Epilogue*: In 1990, van Gogh's *Portrait of Dr. Gachet* sold for $82 million. This was a world record price for a painting.

#TIL 200. The first telephone in the White House was installed during President Rutherford B. Hayes's administration. The installer was Alexander Graham Bell.

#TIL 201. The lifespan of the Greenland shark, an apex predator (no other species preys on it), is between 300 and 500 years. It reaches "shark puberty" at the age of 150. A dead Greenland shark was autopsied and found to have an entire reindeer body in its stomach.

#TIL 202. Stay Puft Marshmallows have 100 mg. of caffeine in each marshmallow.

#TIL 203. Isaac Jogues was a professor of literature and the first Catholic priest to ever set foot on Manhattan Island. During an attempt to convert the Sioux to Christianity, he was captured, tortured, and kept as a slave for thirteen months, during which he was regularly brutalized. After being freed, and a two-month ocean voyage, he celebrated Mass in France with hands that were missing fingers from having been eaten or burned off. He then returned to America as a missionary to the Iroquois, who considered him a sorcerer. Jogues was the one who named Lake George. The Iroquois eventually decapitated him and threw his body into

STEPHEN SPIGNESI — 71

the Mohawk River. He was named a Catholic saint in 1930.

#TIL 204. Every person on earth is every other person's 50th or closer cousin.

#TIL 205. Elton John was the second choice to write the songs for *The Lion King* movie. Their first choice was the group ABBA.

#TIL 206. There is a piece of the Moon embedded in a stained glass window in the Washington National Cathedral. It was presented to the cathedral by the astronauts of *Apollo XI*. The window is known as the "Space Window."

#TIL 207. The rose is the most popular flower in the world. Numbers 2 through 5 are the carnation, tulip, daisy, and sunflower.

#TIL 208. The pink suit Jackie Kennedy was wearing when her husband President Kennedy was assassinated was never cleaned and was donated to the National Archives and Records Administration. It will be placed on public display in 2103.

#TIL 209. The RMS *Titanic* was built by the White Star Line in order to more effectively compete with the Cunard Line. Cunard ultimately bought and absorbed the White Star Line in 1934, twenty-two years after the sinking of the *Titanic*.

#TIL 210. There's a mistake in the beloved Blue Oyster Cult song "Don't Fear the Reaper." The lyrics state that 40,000 men and women died everyday. In July 1976, the actual number of global deaths each day was around 140,000 people.

#TIL 211. On December 16, 1997, 685 people were rushed to the hospital in Japan with epileptic seizures after watching an episode of *Pokémon* called "Electric Soldier Porygon." The episode included a 6-second scene of flashing red and blue lights that triggered the seizures. The episode has never been shown again on Japanese TV but the seizure-inducing scene can be seen on YouTube.

#TIL 212. On March 25, 1911, 146 workers at the Triangle Shirtwaist Factory in New York City died when the factory caught fire and they couldn't escape because all the exit doors were locked.

#TIL 213. Until 2011, Russia classified beer as a "soft drink."

#TIL 214. Meredith Hunter was stabbed to death by a Hell's Angel at the 1969 Altamont

Free Concert. The Rolling Stones were performing, and for years, it was believed that the song they were playing when Hunter was killed was "Sympathy for the Devil." It wasn't. *Rolling Stone* magazine made a mistake when reporting the incident. They were actually playing "Under My Thumb."

#TIL 215. A common pop culture misconception is that Twinkies last for years. They don't. They have a life expectancy of 45 days and are usually on store shelves for between seven and ten days.

#TIL 216. The treatment for a hernia in the 1300s was grotesque. A hernia is a section of organ or muscle pushing through abdominal tissues. The patient would be given enemas and emetics to induce bowel movements and vomiting. The patient was then hung upside down for a few hours and then encased in plaster and strapped to a bed for fifty days.

If the patient survived, there was a possibility the hernia might have reduced.

#TIL 217. The Great Chicago Fire of 1871 was started when Mrs. O'Leary's cow kicked over a lantern, right? Wrong. That story was completely fabricated by a newspaper reporter looking to add some color and drama to his account of the fire.

#TIL 218. The Catholic Church decides if healings that take place after visiting the Lady of Lourdes Shrine in France are actual miracles. In February 2018, the church declared the 70th miraculous Lourdes healing. A 79-year-old nun, wheelchair bound and disabled from spinal troubles, spontaneously stood up from her wheelchair and was able to walk pain free after visiting Lourdes in 2008.

#TIL 219. Martha M. Place was the first woman to die in the electric chair. She was executed for the murder of her stepdaughter Ida. She also tried to kill her husband with an axe but he threw acid in her eyes and escaped death. She was electrocuted on March 20, 1899 at Sing Sing Prison in Ossining, New York.

#TIL 220. Composer Joseph Haydn died in Vienna on May 31, 1809. Shortly after his burial, two men interested in phrenology bribed the gravedigger and stole Haydn's head. The skull wasn't restored to the body until 1954 when the composer's descendant had a crypt built for Haydn and the head was reunited with its owner when the remains were ceremoniously entombed.

#TIL 221. The biggest employer in the United States is Walmart. They employ 1.5 million Americans, and 2.2 million people worldwide.

#TIL 222. "Casual wards" in 18th century English workhouses were dirtier and darker than the rest of the workhouse and were used to house men and women who were essentially irredeemable; i.e. people who weren't looking for work and who wouldn't take a job even if they were offered one. They were believed to be freeloaders wanting to live off others' beneficence.

#TIL 223. The oldest recording of a U.S. president speaking is of Benjamin Harrison, recorded in 1889 or so, opening the Pan-American Congress. He was recorded on an Edison wax cylinder and the recording is on YouTube. He said, "As president of the United States, I was present at the first Pan-American congress in Washington D.C. I believe that with God's help, our two countries shall continue to live side-by-side in peace and prosperity."

#TIL 224. Male athletes in the ancient Greek Olympics competed naked, covered in olive oil.

#TIL 225. President Harry Truman believed in the superiority of women, once writing in a letter to Bess Wallace (his future wife), "I've always thought that the best man in the world is hardly good enough for any woman."

#TIL 226. A typical modern computer mouse has a lifespan of approximately 30 million clicks.

#TIL 227. British politician Winston Churchill's father, Lord Randolph Churchill, died of end-stage syphilis, which included paralysis, insanity, and blindness. Lord Randolph impregnated his wife, Jennie Jerome, when he was infected with disease and, thus, Winston was very lucky he was not born with the birth defects common to children infected with syphilis in the womb.

#TIL 228. There are approximately 500,000 ATM machines in America as of 2019.

#TIL 229. In the Beatles' "Hey Jude," the legendary final "na-na-na" refrain begins at precisely 3:09, the phrase is repeated 18 complete times, and it fades to silence after the beginning of the 19th time. The syllable "na" is repeated 198 times within the 18 complete refrains. Each individual "na-na-na" refrain lasts approximately 13 seconds.

#TIL 230. In 1979, Bruce Jenner appeared in an ad for exercise equipment with the headline, "You may not have Bruce Jenner's body, but you can have his exercise program." In April 2015, Bruce Jenner transitioned to Caitlyn Jenner and no longer had Bruce Jenner's body.

#TIL 231. Hair analysis is no joke: One strand of hair can provide information on everything in your body, including alcohol, drugs of all types, and even vitamins.

#TIL 232. In 2018, according to the FBI, there were 11.67 bank robberies each weekday in the United States, for a total of 3,033 robberies.

#TIL 233. The most-watched TV event in the United States was the *Apollo 11* moon landing on July 20, 1969. It had an estimated viewership of between 125 and 150 million people. The second most-watched TV event was Super Bowl XLIX on February 1, 2015, with 114.14 million viewers. The most-watched TV episode was the *M*A*S*H* finale on February 28, 1983, with 105.9 million viewers. The most-watched "Other" event was President Richard Nixon's resignation speech on August 9, 1974, with 110 million viewers.

#TIL 234. U.S. Founding Father John Witherspoon was the President of Princeton University, a member of the Second Continental Congress, a clergyman, and a theologian. Actress Reese Witherspoon claims descendancy from John Witherspoon but the Witherspoon Foundation said, yes, she's probably related, but not a direct descendant.

#TIL 235. The National Hot Dog and Sausage Council estimates that Americans consume 20 billion hot dogs a year. That's around 55 million hot dogs eaten each and every day.

#TIL 236. U.S. President James Garfield could simultaneously write Greek with one hand and Latin with the other.

#TIL 237. A popular and widely-believed myth in Great Britain is that a pregnant woman can urinate anywhere she wishes, including in a police officer's helmet. This is not true. The Public Order Act of 1986 states that public urination is considered disorderly behavior and the perpetrator (the "pee-pertrator"? Sorry.) can be fined.

#TIL 238. You do not want to be bitten by the Boomslang Snake of sub-Saharan Africa. Its venom causes victims to hemorrhage from every orifice in their body.

#TIL 239. Your heart will beat in time to the music you're listening to.

#TIL 240. Secret Service agents routinely sweep hotel rooms the U.S. president will be staying in for electronic bugs, i.e. listening devices. Sometimes they find bugs intended for the previous guest. Once, when sweeping a hotel room before a Ronald Reagan visit, the Secret Service did, indeed, find a bug that had been placed to eavesdrop on the guest who had recently checked out. The guest? Elton John.

#TIL 241. The resolution of the human eye is 576 megapixels.

#TIL 242. U.S. Founding Father Patrick Henry's wife Sarah developed what would today be diagnosed as a severe mental illness, believed to be puerperal (or postpartum) psychosis, a range of mental illness often following childbirth. Rather than lock her up in a filthy psychiatric "hospital," Patrick built her an apartment and cared for her until her death. After her death, however, Sarah Henry was refused a Christian burial because it was believed her illness was caused by being possessed by the devil.

#TIL 243. One of the longest novels ever written is *Men of Goodwill* by Jules Romains. It consists of twenty-seven volumes and comprises two million words. It has 779 chapters.

#TIL 244. Waterbeds make up only 5 percent of the bed market. Their peak was a 20 percent share of the market in 1986.

#TIL 245. Andrew Johnson and Lyndon Johnson were the only U.S. presidents to suffer from kidney stones. (So far. That we know of.)

#TIL 246. The Moon is shaped like a lemon.

#TIL 247. Anyone can ask to use the Hubble Telescope. The competition is fierce, though, and only one in five astronomers, students, scientists, and other star-gazers get approved for a date with the telescope.

#TIL 248. The Coca-Cola company uses 3.5 million pounds of caffeine a year in their Coke and Diet Coke beverages.

#TIL 249. U.S. President Teddy Roosevelt was merciless—and quite articulate—when he did not like someone. This is how he described President Benjamin Harrison: "A cold-blooded, narrow-minded, prejudiced, obstinate, timid old psalm-singing Indianapolis politician."

#TIL 250. The most popular tourist destination in India in 2019 was not the Taj Mahal. It was the Dharavi Slum in Mumbai. Pictures aren't allowed.

#TIL 251. The world's tallest glass-bottomed bridge is in Zhangjiajie, China; it towers 985 feet above a valley. As a prank, the owners rigged part of the bridge to appear as if the glass was cracking when people walked on it. It did not go over very well and they ultimately apologized for scaring the bejesus out of people.

#TIL 252. A Millennial is someone born between 1981 and 1996 which, in 2020, are people aged 24-39. The American Psychological Association reported in 2018 that Millennials have the highest stress level of any generation.

#TIL 253.   Your skeleton is completely new every ten years.

#TIL 254.   The use of the phrase "a candle in the wind" pre-dates the Elton John song "Candle in the Wind" by sixty-one years. In 1936, American poet Carl Sandburg released the book-length poem, *The People, Yes*, which included the line, "Man's life? A candle in the wind."

#TIL 255.   Calvin Coolidge, the thirtieth U.S. President, liked to have his head rubbed with petroleum jelly while he ate his favorite breakfast, boiled raw wheat and rye, in bed.

#TIL 256.   Doctors can transplant a heart (and a slew of other organs), but they still can't transplant an eyeball. Modern medicine is not yet capable of reconstructing the highly complex optic nerve, which connects the eye to the brain.

#TIL 257. The Pony Express, which replaced stagecoach delivery of mail after the Gold Rush of 1848, only lasted eighteen months. Eventually the telegraph and the start of the Civil War contributed to it ceasing operations.

#TIL 258. The shortest recorded war in history was the Anglo-Zanzibar War of 1896. It was between the British forces occupying Zanzibar and the Zanzibar armies. It lasted between 38 and 45 minutes. (The British won.)

#TIL 259. In 1943, IBM chairman Thomas Watson said, "I think there is a world market for maybe five computers."

#TIL 260. You are not allowed to touch the Queen of England. You are permitted to shake her hand, but only if she offers her hand to you.

#TIL 261. Cruise ships are required to have morgues and to carry body bags. According to the cruise ship industry, 200 people die each year on cruises and the ships store the bodies until they reach their next port where they are unloaded and a death certificate is issued. Plans are then made for shipping the deceased to wherever their final remains are to be dealt with. Interestingly, in the past twenty years, 284 people have also fallen off cruise ships. Most of the time their bodies are recovered, but their deaths are not counted in the annual total of "deaths onboard." The cruise ship industry says people don't fall off cruise ships if they behave responsibly.

#TIL 262. Leonardo Da Vinci's *Codex Leicester* is a 72-page scientific notebook that covers a variety of topics, including astronomy, water movement, fossils, and lunar reflection. In 1884, Bill Gates purchased the book for $32.5

million. It is currently the most expensive book ever sold.

#TIL 263. In 2010, a 300-foot-deep sinkhole appeared in Guatemala and swallowed a three-story factory whole. The cause was water leakage from sewers as well as a tropical storm.

#TIL 264. In 1959, IBM issued a statement to a group of investors who were in the process of founding the Xerox company. IBM said, "The world potential market for copying machines is 5,000 at most."

#TIL 265. William Safire wrote a speech for President Nixon in the event astronauts Neil Armstrong and Buzz Aldrin couldn't get off the Moon. This is that speech:

Fate has ordained that the men who went to the moon to explore in peace will stay on the moon to rest in peace. These brave men, Neil Armstrong and Edwin Aldrin, know that there is no hope for their recovery. But they also know that there is hope for mankind in their sacrifice. These two men are laying down their lives in mankind's most noble goal: the search for truth and understanding. They will be mourned by their families and friends; they will be mourned by their nation; they will be mourned by the people of the world; they will be mourned by a Mother Earth that dared send two of her sons into the unknown. In their exploration, they stirred the people of the world to feel as one; in their sacrifice, they bind more tightly the brotherhood of man. In ancient days, men looked at stars and saw their heroes in the constellations. In modern times, we do much the same, but our heroes are epic men of flesh and blood. Others will follow, and surely find their way home. Man's search will not be denied. But these men were the first, and they will remain the foremost in our hearts. For every human being who looks up at the moon in the nights to come will know *that there is some corner of another world that is forever mankind.*

After The President's Statement, At The Point When NASA Ends Communications With The Men:

A clergyman should adopt the same procedure as a burial at sea, commending their souls to "the deepest of the deep," concluding with the Lord's Prayer.

#TIL 266. The original name of the game *Operation* was *Death Valley.*

#TIL 267. From the Council of Nicaea in 787 until 1969, the Catholic church decreed that every Catholic church had to have a relic of a saint on its premises, oftentimes in the altar. This practice was stopped in 1969, but there is still a thriving market for body parts and possessions of saints. The A. R. Broomer antiques shop in New York City traffics in relics and has the vertebrae of 6th century martyr

St. Redempta. They come with papers and a papal wax seal, and sell for $2,500.

#TIL 268. John F. Kennedy was diagnosed with Addison's disease when he was thirty years old and given a year to live. Addison's disease is also known as adrenal insufficiency. JFK took steroids all his life until his assassination in 1963.

#TIL 269. The mayfly has the shortest life expectancy of any creature on earth: it is born, lives, reproduces, and dies within 24 hours.

#TIL 270. Legendary painter Bob Ross filmed 403 episodes of his beloved show, *The Joy of Painting*. He painted three paintings for each show: one as a reference painting before the show; one during the show; and then a third for his "how-to" books. These paintings all still exist but are not for sale nor available for viewing by his fans and the public.

#TIL 271. The S.E.A. Aquarium in Singapore is the world's largest aquarium. It holds 11.3 million gallons of water. It is home to 80,000 animals comprising 800 species.

#TIL 272. Franklin D. Roosevelt did not contract polio until he was thirty-nine years old. The disease caused permanent paralysis in both legs. He was elected President of the United States twelve years later in 1933. It is estimated that of the 125,000 photos of FDR in the FDR Presidential Library, two are of the President sitting in his wheelchair.

#TIL 273. One of the most persistent superstitions in modern culture is fear of Friday the 13th. This fear is called paraskevidekatriaphobia. Stephen King reportedly suffers from this, although his fear is more generally fear of the number thirteen, which is called triskaidekaphobia.

#TIL 274. According to the New England Historic Genealogical Society, President Barack Obama is actor Brad Pitt's ninth cousin, and Vice President Dick Cheney's eighth cousin.

#TIL 275. A human being can live a normal life without these organs: one lung, one kidney, gallbladder, appendix, tonsils, adenoids, spleen, uterus, ovaries, breasts, testicles, eyes, stomach, colon, many bones, and the larynx.

#TIL 276. The Jim Twins were twin brothers born in 1940 and immediately separated and adopted by two different families. They did not see each other again for thirty-nine years. When they reunited in 1979, they discovered that their adoptive parents had named each of them Jim, and that each brother had married twice. Each of their first wives was named Linda and each of their second wives was named Betty. They each had a son. The sons were named

James Allen and James Alan. They each had a dog named Toy. They had each worked as a sheriff's deputy, they drank the same brand of beer, and they both owned Chevrolets.

#TIL 277. There are more than 100 discarded objects, including golf balls, on the Moon. There is also what is considered an art object— and it's the only *objet d'art* on the surface of the Moon. It is a 3.3 inch square piece of aluminum called *Fallen Astronaut* that bears the names of fourteen astronauts and cosmonauts who died during their service in their countries' space programs.

#TIL 278. Some of the best-selling books in literary history struggled to find a publisher and were repeatedly rejected, including *Anne of Green Gables, Chicken Soup for the Soul, Zen and the Art of Motorcycle Maintenance, The Help, Carrie, A Time to Kill, A Wrinkle in Time, Dune, Catch-22, Lord of the Flies, The*

Diary of Anne Frank, Gone With the Wind, Watership Down, M*A*S*H, and *Lolita.*

#TIL 279. In 2014, China produced 58 percent of the world's peaches and nectarines.

#TIL 280. Samuel J. Seymour witnessed President Abraham Lincoln's assassination when he was five years old and lived long enough to appear on February 9, 1956 on the TV game show *I've Got a Secret.* His secret, of course, was that he had been in Ford's Theater on the night of April 14, 1865, when Lincoln was shot. The panel guessed his secret. Seymour died two months later.

#TIL 281. On January 20, 1936, Britain's King George V, who was lying in his bed in a coma, was euthanized by his physician with 750 milligrams of morphine and 1,000 milligrams of cocaine at 11:00 at night so his death could be reported in the morning papers.

The evening papers weren't considered significant enough to report a monarch's demise. In his notes, the good doctor even admitted to performing the injections so the king's death could be announced "in the morning papers rather than the less appropriate evening journals."

#TIL 282. Do you like the 1925 movie *Ben-Hur*? If you're an animal lover you might want to reconsider your affection for the classic flick. The producers killed 100 horses during the making of the movie, mainly by tripping galloping steeds with a wire so that they would fall on camera. This usually resulted in broken legs which required euthanizing the animal. In 1997, the film was selected for preservation in the United States National Film Registry by the Library of Congress as being "culturally, historically, or aesthetically significant."

#TIL 283. According to the United States Department of Agriculture, the potato is America's most popular vegetable, followed by the tomato. (America's adoration of and obsession with pizza and french fries is why.)

#TIL 284. The CBS series *Northern Exposure* was set in the fictitious small town of Cicely, Alaska, and filmed in the very real, very small town (4.37 square miles according to the US Census Bureau) of Roslyn, Washington. The show brought eleven new businesses to the town, created more than 100 new jobs, and increased tax revenue to Roslyn by 30 percent. When the show was cancelled by CBS in 1995, Roslyn re-defined itself as a tourist attraction geared to *Northern Exposure* fans and many local businesses use that connection as a draw for fans from all over the world.

#TIL 285. Neil Armstrong carried pieces of the Wright Brothers' first plane onboard the *Apollo 11* flight to the Moon.

#TIL 286. Leo Tolstoy hated the writings of William Shakespeare. He said he felt an "irresistible repulsion and tedium" when he read the work of the Bard of Avon.

#TIL 287. According to HealthGrades.com, the most common surgical procedure performed in the United States is cataract removal. Number 2 is Caesarean section, and number 3 is joint replacement.

#TIL 288. In New Hampshire, it's against the law to have a picnic in a cemetery.

#TIL 289. U.S. President Franklin Pierce and American novelist Nathaniel Hawthorne were best friends. Pierce was with Hawthorne at the Pemigewasset House in Plymouth, Massachusetts, when Hawthorne died in his sleep.

#TIL 290. Buddha was not fat, all the statuary depictions of him notwithstanding. He was depicted as a roly-poly character because being fat symbolized being happy in the East.

#TIL 291. According to the Global Footprint Network, on July 29, 2019, 209 days into 2019, mankind consumed the whole year's worth of Earth's natural resources. These include water, food, timber, land, carbon, and other natural resources. At this rate, we need 1.75 Earths to break even and consume resources at a rate at which the planet can replenish them. Each year, the date on which we go into "resources debt," so to speak, is called Earth Overshoot Day.

#TIL 292. According to research published in the *Research in Transportation Economics* journal, there is one fatality for every 16 million airline flights. It's a cliché but it's true: airplane crashes are such a big subject when they happen because of how infrequently they happen.

#TIL 293. The Apollo Guidance Computer that landed U.S. astronauts on the Moon and returned them safely to Earth had the computing power equivalent to a pocket calculator of today.

#TIL 294. In the mid-1890s, New York City Chief of Police Theodore Roosevelt (yes, the future president) declared war on banana peels because too many people were slipping on them and sustaining injuries, many of which were often serious. At the time, people discarded their banana peels in the street and on the sidewalks. He gave a talk to his officers on "the bad habits of the banana skin, dwelling particularly on its tendency to toss people into the air and bring them down with terrific force on the hard pavement."

#TIL 295. For his 1984 movie *Moscow on the Hudson*, Robin Williams learned to speak Russian and play the saxophone. Native Russian speakers said that Robin spoke the language without any accent whatsoever, and saxophone players said Robin was able to play at a 2-year proficiency level.

#TIL 296. During World War II, Japanese soldiers ate the flesh of captured enemy soldiers to prevent starvation. There was actually a memo that prohibited the soldiers cannibalizing anyone but the enemy.

#TIL 297. According to Google, the most misspelled word in the state of Wisconsin is "Wisconsin."

#TIL 298. According to the *New York Times*, "your odds of getting into Harvard or Stanford are higher than your chances of being accepted as a donor at the major sperm banks." Some of the criteria that will destroy a man's chances of getting accepted include being white and short (under 5'9" is a non-starter; there's some flexibility for other ethnicities), low sperm count, bad health, being an Ashkenazi Jew (they have a high number of genetic diseases, including Tay-Sachs disease, Canavan disease, cystic fibrosis, and familial dysautonomia), and the inability to donate at least once a week for six months to a year (with three days of abstinence prior to each donation). Typically, two donations a week will earn the donor about $1,500 a month, which averages out to just under $200 per donation.

#TIL 299.   Mono (mononucleosis)—the "kissing disease"—is not highly contagious, despite the common belief that it is.

#TIL 300.   When President Bill Clinton tore a tendon in his knee in 1997 and needed surgery, dozens of surgeons participated in the routine surgical procedure, so each one could say they operated on the president of the United States. The result was that the simple operation took hours.

#TIL 301.   Lawn darts are illegal in the United States.

#TIL 302.   In the third-season episode of the TV series *Younger*, called "A Night at the Opera," Maggie and Lauren talk about how their periods finally synced up after living together for a while. Scientific studies, however, have shown that period syncing is mostly coincidence and that if two women live together long enough, their periods will coincide simply because of the vagaries of the length of a menstrual cycle and the calendar.

#TIL 303. To be sure that the cyanide capsules he wanted to use to commit suicide would do the job, Adolf Hitler fed one to his dog Blondi, who died shortly thereafter. According to historian James O'Donnell, Hitler was extremely bereft due to the death of his dog. Whom he killed.

#TIL 304. The majority of genetic diseases—diseases caused by one or more abnormalities in a person's genes—are incurable.

#TIL 305. In July 2019, a seven-year-old boy in India complained of jaw pain. After X-rays, doctors surgically removed a sac filled with 526 teeth that had been embedded in his lower jaw. The rare condition is known as compound composite odontoma. There's no known confirmed cause for the condition and doctors think it could be genetic.

#TIL 306. One of Abraham Lincoln's most memorable quotes on slavery was, "Whenever I hear anyone arguing for slavery, I feel a strong impulse to have it tried on him personally."

#TIL 307. Americans eat 150 million hot dogs on the Fourth of July, according to the National Hot Dog and Sausage Council.

#TIL 308. There are between 5,000 and 10,000 bodies buried beneath the New Haven Green in New Haven, Connecticut. The headstones were moved but the bodies were left in place.

#TIL 309. Ad-libbed lines from movies that became extremely famous include "Here's looking at you, kid," ad-libbed by Humphrey Bogart in 1942's *Casablanca*; "I'm walkin' here!", ad-libbed by Dustin Hoffman in 1969's *Midnight Cowboy*; "You talkin' to me?", ad-libbed by Robert De Niro in 1976's *Taxi Driver*; "You're gonna need a bigger boat," ad-libbed by Roy Scheider in 1975's *Jaws*; "I'm a zit. Get it?", ad-libbed by John Belushi in 1978's *Animal House*; and "Here's Johnny!", ad-libbed by Jack Nicholson in 1980's *The Shining*.

#TIL 310. The original Barbie doll sold for $3.00. Today that doll is worth around $25,000.

#TIL 311. John Hinckley, Jr., the Oklahoma man who tried to assassinate President Ronald Reagan in 1981, is out of custody and living on his own. Conditions of his release include not owning guns, not drinking alcohol, not talking to the press, not watching porn, not deleting his browser history, not listening to music that encourages violence, not driving more than thirty miles from his mother's home, seeing a psychiatrist twice a month, and working three days a week.

#TIL 312. The results of polygraph tests are not admissible in court. They're too inaccurate to be 100 percent reliable.

#TIL 313. There is ongoing debate as to whether or not a decapitated head retains consciousness. Some scientists believe that since there is no trauma to the brain during a clean decapitation (as with a guillotine or surgically sharp sword, for example) it is possible that oxygen can continue to keep the brain functioning for a period of time. Some suggest up to four seconds; some say as much as twenty-nine seconds. There are historical accounts of heads grimacing and changing expressions after being decapitated. Alan Bellows, in his 2006 article "Lucid Decapitation," reported the 1989 story of an Army veteran who was in a car accident with a friend who was decapitated. The man claimed his friend's expression visibly changed for several seconds, "first of shock or confusion then to terror or grief."

#TIL 314. The naked baby on the cover of the Nirvana *Nevermind* album is Spencer Elden, who was four months old when he was photographed for the record. Elden is now twenty-five and he recreated the shot, this time wearing swim trunks, in 2016, to celebrate the classic album's twenty-fifth anniversary.

#TIL 315. Misophonia is a psychological disorder in which people become agitated, angry, upset, or panicked when they hear certain ordinary sounds. Included in the roster of sounds that trigger people with the condition are chewing noises, breathing sounds, typing sounds, tapping sounds, and even the repetitive sound of windshield wipers.

#TIL 316. The Apple end-user license agreement has a clause in it that states that anyone who buys an App from the Apple Store will "not use [it] for . . . the development, design, manufacture, or production of nuclear, missile, or chemical or biological weapons."

#TIL 317. A very popular color in Paris during the Victorian era was emerald green, also known as "Paris green." It was widely used in France and England, until someone figured out that it was killing people. Paris green was made by mixing copper and arsenic. Napoleon's doctor visited the workshop where the dye was made and saw many workers in the end stages of arsenic poisoning. After he reported his findings, the dye was banned.

#TIL 318. There is a Disgusting Food Museum in Malmö, Sweden. Some of the foods on display include *Casu marzu*, which is maggot-infested cheese from Sardinia; lamprey pie; nests made from bird saliva; tree-ant larvae; and rotten shark, which is a delicacy in Iceland. On the museum's website, the Museum's Director and Curator report on the most disgusting thing they've ever eaten. For Director Andreas Ahrens, it was the aforementioned rotten shark. For Curator and Chief Disgustologist Samuel West, it was a duck fetus cooked in its egg.

#TIL 319. Famous Depression-era bank robber John Dillinger was buried in 1934 after being shot dead by the Feds. In August 2019, his niece and nephew announced plans to exhume his body for DNA testing because they don't believe the man buried in Dillinger's grave is their uncle.

#TIL 320. There's a road on a mountain in La Paz, Bolivia known as the Death Road. It's fifty miles long, has no guardrails or safety features and, usually, 200 to 300 people a year die from falling off the road. One year a tourist bus went over the side, killing the driver. Fifty passengers had wisely de-bussed prior to the accident.

#TIL 321. Panspermia is the astrobiological theory that life exists everywhere in the universe and that life on earth could have originated from microorganisms or chemical precursors of life present in outer space and able to initiate life on reaching a suitable environment via meteor crashes on the surface of the planet.

#TIL 322. At Best Buy, a price ending in ".92" means that the product has been marked down once, sometimes below wholesale cost, and that it's a great deal. At Home Depot, a price ending in ".06" means that the item is on sale and that the price will drop again in six weeks.

#TIL 323. Brian May is an astrophysicist who worked on New Horizons, the first space mission to explore the planet Pluto. May is also the lead guitarist for Queen.

#TIL 324. In Ancient Rome and Greece, men held their penises like a cigarette when urinating. Modern men hold it like a laser pointer. This was because the ancient Roman and Greek men wanted their penis to appear smaller because a smaller organ was considered aesthetically beautiful. (Thanks to *The History Girls* blog for this penile factoid.)

#TIL 325. A guy named Donald Gorske from Fond du Lac, Wisconsin, is the Guinness Book of World Records holder for most Big Macs consumed. He eats two a day and on August 24, 2016, he ate his 28,788th Big Mac, winning the record. And the thing is, he doesn't even eat them fresh. He buys them in bulk and then microwaves them at home.

#TIL 326. There are two glacial islands in Antarctica named "The Office Girls." Reportedly this was done as a tribute to the legion of U.S. female office workers who catalogued

for posterity all the myriad tiny pieces of
Antarctica.

#TIL 327. A novella called *Futility* by Morgan Robertson
was published in 1898, fourteen years before
the sinking of the *Titanic*. In *Futility*, the ship
the *Titan*, the largest ship ever built, sinks on
its maiden voyage. (After the sinking of the
Titanic, *Futility* was reissued as *The Wreck of
the Titan*.)

#TIL 328. The U.S. Army Corps of Engineers owns a
massive collection of fossils, all of which were
uncovered while working on flood control
projects across the United States.

#TIL 329. The Bibliothéque National de France in Paris
is the national library of France. It is believed
to house the world's largest collection of
pornography and erotica. The nickname of
the basement chamber where the lascivious

livres live is *"L'enfer"*, which is French for "hell."

#TIL 330. The Great Stink was an event that occurred in July and August of 1858 in London, England. The extremely hot temperatures of those months caused untreated human waste and outflowings from factories to reek to high heaven, so to speak, as well as cause a cholera outbreak. The Great Stink spurred the creation and construction of pumping stations, and a drainage system that ultimately alleviated the problem.

#TIL 331. Led Zeppelin guitarist Jimmy Page is reputed to own 1,500 guitars but this number has never been conclusively confirmed. It can be said, though, that Page owns so many guitars that even if the number might be off a tad, that does not minimize the massive size of his collection.

#TIL 332. Two of the weirdest phobias are spectrophobia and linonophobia. Spectrophobia is the fear of mirrors and your own reflection. Linonophobia is the fear of string.

#TIL 333. In the eighteenth and nineteenth centuries, dentures were commonly made using the teeth of dead soldiers. This started in 1815 after the French lost the Battle of Waterloo. The teeth extracted from the dead after that battle became known as Waterloo Teeth.

#TIL 334. Elton John does not have a piano in his London mansion. In 2016, a UK *Guardian* journalist visited Elton's home and was surprised that there were no pianos in the house. Elton explained: "I play 107 shows a year, why am I going to go home and play the fucking piano? . . . God, I couldn't think of anything worse. I have leisure, and I have work. And I do enough work. When I get home, the last thing I want to do is play the piano."

#TIL 335. Lynching postcards (exactly what you think they are) were sold in the United States for more than fifty years until they were banned by the Comstock Act in 1908.

#TIL 336. In July 2019, a massive swarm of grasshoppers descended on Las Vegas. There were so many grasshoppers, they were visible on weather radar from above the city.

#TIL 337. On April 30, 2008, magician David Blaine held his breath on *The Oprah Winfrey Show* for 17 minutes and 4 seconds, breaking the world record. He did it by practicing a technique called glossopharyngeal insufflation, also known as "lung packing." This method maximizes the amount of air he could hold in his lungs, and is a practice deep divers use for extremely deep descents.

#TIL 338. *Swann's Way*, the first volume of Marcel Proust's seven-volume epic *Remembrance of Things Past* (known in French as *In Search of Lost Time*) was self-published after the novel was repeatedly rejected by publishers.

#TIL 339. On July 29, 2019, Ethiopia planted more than 350 million trees in twelve hours to combat climate change and Ethiopia's drastic deforestation problem.

#TIL 340. On Tuesday, July 30, 2019, a first edition of J. K. Rowling's *Harry Potter and the Philosopher's Stone* sold at auction for $34,500. The reasons for the high price are twofold. Only 500 copies of the book were printed and, more importantly, the book contained two typos. The word "Philosopher" was misspelled in the back cover copy as "Philospher." And the term "1 wand" was repeated twice on page 53 in a list titled "Other Equipment."

#TIL 341. The first underwater footage was taken by J.E. Williamson in 1914 and featured Williamson stabbing a shark to death. He had to promise a fight between a man and a shark to convince his investors to fund the project.

#TIL 342. Flying is the safest mode of transportation on earth. Riding a motorcycle is the most dangerous.

#TIL 343. Arlington National Cemetery is located on the estate of Confederate General Robert E. Lee, from whom it was confiscated after the Civil War. Buried at the cemetery are the bodies of 4,000 freed slaves, three enemy combatants, and soldiers from every war in U.S. history.

#TIL 344. NASA's name and logo are public domain and can be used commercially for free.

#TIL 345. The advertising campaign that became known as the worst sales promotion in history destroyed the Hoover vacuum company. The company offered two free round-trip tickets to New York or New Orleans if a customer bought more than $250 (100 UK pounds at the time) worth of Hoover products. They lost around 570 pounds per sale ($1,400) and three years later sold the company to an Italian concern at a loss of $81 million.

#TIL 346. A coal vein beneath Centralia, Pennsylvania, was accidentally set on fire in May 1962. The coal has been burning ever since and is expected to continue to burn for another 250 years. Seven people still live in Centralia. They went to court to be allowed to stay. They can't sell or pass down their land and after they're gone, their houses will be demolished.

#TIL 347. The band Toto played the music on Michael Jackson's 1982 album *Thriller*.

#TIL 348. People who eat a lot of garlic will smell like garlic. The allicin compound in the vegetable is absorbed and combines with bacteria that oozes from the skin as perspiration. Thus, garlic-stinking people.

#TIL 349. According to Major League Baseball, ninety baseballs are required at the beginning of every game. Between sixty and seventy baseballs are used per game. The average major league baseball is replaced after approximately six pitches.

#TIL 350. According to Michael Slater, emeritus professor of Victorian literature at Birkbec, University of London, and author of the biography, *Charles Dickens*, it is likely Dickens had obsessive compulsive disorder

(OCD). He would neurotically rearrange the furniture in hotel rooms to meet his requirements, and also manifested other symptoms recognizable today as indicators of the condition.

#TIL 351. Cats can't taste sweet foods. They're lacking the amino acids needed to do so.

#TIL 352. According to the Beaumont Emergency Center in Beaumont, Texas, the most common reason people visit an Emergency Department is headaches. Number two is foreign objects in the body; number three is skin infections; number four is back pain; number five is contusions and cuts; number six is upper respiratory infections; number seven is broken bones and sprains; number eight is toothaches; number nine is abdominal pains; and number ten is chest pains.

#TIL 353.   According to the chess website thechessworld.com, the longest possible chess game would consist of 5,949 moves. The longest game ever played consisted of 269 moves . . . and ended in a draw!

#TIL 354.   Def Leppard has a one-armed drummer, Rick Allen. He uses his left foot to "stomp" on specially designed pedals that strike the drums, replacing the action of his left hand. He lost his arm in a car accident in 1985, and even though it was reattached, it had to be re-amputated due to an infection. The pop culture website PPcorn.com named Rick Allen the fourth greatest drummer on their "Top 10 Drummers of All Time" list.

#TIL 355.   The country with the lowest divorce rate in the world is India, at 1%. The highest is Luxembourg, at 87%.

#TIL 356.   In 2003, a United States poster company airbrushed the cigarette out of Paul McCartney's hand for their poster of the *Abbey Road* album cover. At the time, an Apple spokesman said, "We have never agreed to anything like this. It seems these poster companies got a little carried away. They shouldn't have done what they have, but there isn't much we can do about it now." The poster came out fourteen months after George Harrison's death from cancer, which he believed was caused by him smoking for much of his life. Obviously, the poster company wanted a less politically incorrect image for their poster.

#TIL 357.   In 2013, Goodreads surveyed its members as to the classic book they had abandoned without finishing reading. The number one abandoned book was *Catch-22* by Joseph Heller. Number two was *The Lord of the Rings* by J.R.R. Tolkien; number three was

Ulysses by James Joyce; number four was *Moby-Dick* by Herman Melville; and number five was *Atlas Shrugged* by Ayn Rand.

#TIL 358. At the Museum of Death in Hollywood, the largest display is about Charles Manson. The museum building was once a recording studio where Pink Floyd recorded *The Wall*.

#TIL 359. The late theoretical physicist Stephen Hawking believed that there was the possibility that we would be contacted by alien beings at some point in our future and that, if we were, we shouldn't answer back. "Meeting an advanced civilization could be like Native Americans encountering Columbus. That didn't turn out so well," he said in a documentary in 2016.

#TIL 360. There is a phobia for fear of long words. It is called hippopotomonstrosesquippedaliophobia.

#TIL 361. Lyndon Johnson was the only U.S. president to be sworn in on an airplane. His first presidential order was "Let's get airborne."

#TIL 362. In 1900, the Lloyd Manufacturing Company ran a print ad for their "Cocaine Toothache Drops." They cost fifteen cents and the ad promised, "Instantaneous Cure!"

#TIL 363. Legendary scientist Marie Curie, who discovered polonium and proved that uranium was radioactive, died in 1934 of aplastic anemia caused by her exposure to radiation throughout her life. Her belongings and notes, and her body itself, are still radioactive and will likely remain so for at least another 1,500 years. Researcher who want to work with her notebooks have to sign a waiver and wear full radiation protective gear.

#TIL 364. It is easier to get in to Harvard, which has a 4.5 percent admission rate than to get a job at Walmart, which has a 2.6 percent acceptance rate.

#TIL 365. The now-iconic line "Leave the gun, take the cannoli" in *The Godfather* was originally just "Leave the gun." The "take the cannoli" part was ad-libbed during the scene by actor Richard Castellano (he played Clemenza) and Francis Ford Coppola liked it enough to leave it in the final cut.

#TIL 366. It is estimated that there are 10 quadrillion ants on planet earth. A quadrillion is a 10 followed by fifteen zeroes. There's ten of them of ants.

#TIL 367. The most mentioned person in the Quran by reference is Jesus Christ. He is mentioned, both directly and indirectly, over 187 times.

#TIL 368. An "earworm" is a song that gets stuck in your head that you can't seem to stop hearing. "Baby Shark" is a current example for those of you with kids. According to the pop culture website popculturemadness.com, the most insidious earworm song is Disney's "It's a Small World," followed by The Beatles' "Yellow Submarine," and the theme to *The Andy Griffith Show*. The Top Five are rounded out by Carly Rae Jepson's "Call Me Maybe" at number four and Sonny and Cher's "I Got You Babe" at number five.

#TIL 369. During its heyday as a prison in the 1950s, Alcatraz had to have a million gallons of freshwater shipped in every week because of its saltwater-based island location.

#TIL 370. The Bic Cristal ballpoint pen is made by the Biro Company. It is the best-selling ballpoint pen in history. They sell 14 million of them every day, which is over 5 billion a year.

#TIL 371.   John Kellogg, founder of the Battle Creek Sanitarium and inventor of the cornflake, offered a number of treatments at his clinic in addition to eating cornflakes. These included shooting electricity into a patient's eyeballs and administering 15-quart enemas.

#TIL 372.   The yellow arrow in the Amazon logo is actually a subtle statement that the company sells everything "from A to Z." The arrow begins under the "A" and ends under the "Z."

#TIL 373.   The Woodstock music festival in August 1969 was never intended to be a free event. When 400,000 people showed up—300,000 more than the number of tickets sold—the festival became free for all and, some say, a free-for-all.

#TIL 374. According to the global brand consultancy company Interbrand, the ten most successful global brands are Apple, Google, Coca Cola, Microsoft, Toyota, IBM, Samsung, Amazon, Mercedes-Benz, and General Electric.

#TIL 375. One quarter of all the bones in your body are in your feet (assuming you have two feet, at 26 bones per foot.).

#TIL 376. According to National Public Radio (NPR), the United States spends 2.5 times as much on healthcare per person as does the United Kingdom. Americans also see a physician much less often than people in other countries. Americans see a doctor four times a year; the Japanese see their doctor, on average, monthly.

#TIL 377. The largest paper clip ever made measured 22 feet, 11 inches long and weighed 1,327 pounds. It was made of iron and was put on display in Oslo, Norway, in 1989.

#TIL 378. In America, authors do not earn royalties when their books are checked out from a public library. In the UK and Ireland, they do. Authors there are annually paid an amount calculated based on how many times their books are checked out.

#TIL 379. According to the BBC, there are 96 packets of human excrement, urine, and vomit on the Moon. They were left behind by the 12 Apollo astronauts who visited on the lunar surface.

#TIL 380. Americans throw away 25 percent of the country's food supply—28 billion pounds— every year.

#TIL 381. According to Nancy Brook, nurse practitioner and educator at Stanford Hospital, one of the most important things she would want hospital patients to know is that "Nurses aren't maids." Nor are they waiters or waitresses. (And that all hospitals are understaffed.)

#TIL 382. After George Washington was elected President, Congress came up with the following title for him, which Washington immediately rejected: "His Highness, the President of the United States of America, and Protector of the Rights of Same."

#TIL 383. Naples was the most bombed city In Italy during World War II.

#TIL 384. The banana is both a fruit and a berry.

#TIL 385. No one really knows the identity of the girl in Johannes Vermeer's iconic painting *Girl with a Pearl Earring*. There have been two fictionalized tellings of the girl's story—a novella by Marta Morazzoni called *Girl*

With a Turban in 1986, and the novel *Girl with a Pearl Earring* by Tracey Chevalier in 1999—but the girl's identity has never been confirmed. Other paintings by Vermeer with his daughter as the subject suggest a resemblance to the *Earring* girl, but this is still speculation.

#TIL 386. The last Thursday of every February is National Toast Day. Some people really love toast, and this is their day.

#TIL 387. According to a study titled "Scientific Analysis Reveals Major Differences in the Breast Size of Women in Different Countries," which was published in *The Journal of Female Health Sciences*, women in the United States have the largest breasts in the world.

#TIL 388. In 1967, legendary rock icon Frank Zappa appeared in a derogatory print ad for

Hagstrom acoustic guitars. He posed with the guitar and the copy line read, "Folk rock is a drag." This was the only ad he ever appeared in and he is on record later admitting that he regretted doing it.

#TIL 389. The first cellphone, a Motorola, cost $4,000 (about $10,000 in today's dollars) when it came out in 1983. The first VHS VCR came out in 1977 and cost $1,280 ($4,600 in today's dollars). The first microwave for home use came out in 1955 and cost $1,295 (more than $12,000 in today's dollars).

#TIL 390. The working title of The Beatles song "Yesterday" was "Scrambled Eggs."

#TIL 391. The program that teaches Navy pilots to fly fighter jets is called the United States Navy Strike Fighter Tactics Instructor program. It is popularly known as TOPGUN. Anyone in the program who references or quotes the Tom Cruise movie *Top Gun* must pay a fine of $5.

#TIL 392. The geographic center of the contiguous United States is 2.6 miles north of Lebanon, Kansas at 39°50′N latitude and 98°35′W longitude.

#TIL 393. Italian monk Guido d'Arezzo invented the musical staff around the year 1000 and created what ultimately became today's system of musical notation in his treatise *Micrologus*, around 1026.

#TIL 394. It is illegal to swim in the canals of Venice, Italy.

#TIL 395. The TV series *Breaking Bad* depicted 271 murders and deaths in five seasons, 201 of which were either committed by or connected to Walter "Heisenberg" White. Donald Margolis, Jane's father, was connected to the 167 deaths from the Wayfarer 515 and JM 21 in-flight plane collision; Gustavo Fring was responsible for 27 deaths; Uncle Jack's white supremacist crew was responsible for 23 deaths, and the Salamanca cousins were responsible for 16 deaths.

#TIL 396. Connecticut was the first state to issue permanent license plates for cars. They passed the law requiring plates in 1937.

#TIL 397. Galileo Galilei developed and perfected the Scientific Methods, which is still the gold standard for proving a scientific principle. The six steps of the Scientific Method are: 1. Make an Observation, 2. Form a Question, 3. Form a Hypothesis, 4. Conduct an Experiment, 5. Analyze the Data, and 6. Draw a Conclusion.

#TIL 398. After America won the Revolutionary War, 60,000 loyalists to the King fled the United States and settled in other British territories. More than half went to Nova Scotia, New Brunswick, and Quebec. Some went to Jamaica and the Bahamas (bringing 15,000 slaves with them), some joined the East India Company army, including two sons of Benedict Arnold. Around twelve hundred moved to Africa, and established Freetown in Sierra Leone.

#TIL 399. The Nobel Prize in Literature 1953 was awarded to Winston Churchill "for his mastery of historical and biographical description as well as for brilliant oratory in defending exalted human values."

#TIL 400. John F. Kennedy failed two physicals when he attempted to join the Army and the Navy. He had both physical and gastrointestinal problems, but his powerful father Joe

Kennedy pulled some strings and got him into the Navy in 1941. He became commander of the patrol torpedo boat *PT-109* and saved his crew when the boat was torpedoed in 1943. He ultimately received acclaim as a war hero, even though the military initially rejected him.

#TIL 401. Black licorice, blueberries, iron supplements, and Pepto-Bismol will turn your stool black.

#TIL 402. Kurt Cobain overdosed on heroin the day of a Nirvana concert in July 1983. Courtney Love gave him an injection of the opioid overdose reversal drug Narcan and punched him in the chest. Cobain recovered and performed that night just fine.

#TIL 403. Ontario, Canada, is the world's largest producer of ginseng.

#TIL 404. At the 2010 MTV Music Awards, Lady Gaga wore a meat dress. She said she wore it as a statement that everyone should fight for what they believe in, and as a protest against the Army's "Don't Ask, Don't Tell" policy. The dress was later treated so that it became a kind of beef jerky and is now on display at the Rock and Roll Hall of Fame in Cleveland.

#TIL 405. Death Valley, in California, is the hottest and driest place in America. Summer temps can be greater than 200 degrees Fahrenheit.

#TIL 406. In 1910, a print ad ran in newspapers and magazines for a device called The Recto Rotor. The device was "in a class by itself" and was hailed as a cure for "Piles, Constipation, and Prostate Trouble." It looked like a six-inch long butt plug with a round base. It had "Lubricating Vent Holes" and an "Unguent Chamber" and was advertised as "the only device that reaches the Vital Spot effectively."

#TIL 407. Connecticut never ratified the 18th Amendment, which established Prohibition. Neither did Rhode Island.

#TIL 408. In Florida, there's a law against singing while wearing a bathing suit.

#TIL 409. The ideas for Google, the double helix structure of DNA, and the sewing machine came to their creators (Larry Page, James Watson, and Elisa Howe, respectively) in a dream.

#TIL 410. In the United States, the national sport is Baseball. The national game of Cuba is Dominoes. In Australia, the national sport is Cricket. In Japan, the national sport is Sumo Wrestling. In Turkey, the national sport is Oil Wrestling.

#TIL 411. Members of the National Guard have to swear allegiance to two constitutions: the federal constitution and the constitution of the state in which they're serving.

#TIL 412. Leonardo da Vinci designed the helicopter, the parachute, and the tank centuries before they were invented.

#TIL 413. Classical Languages Professor William Berg translated jokes from what is believed to be the oldest anthology of jokes in existence, the *Philogelos*, which dates from fourth or fifth century Greece. This is one of the more notable knee-slappers from the collection: "Two lazy-bones are fast asleep. A thief comes in, pulls the blanket from the bed, and makes off with it. One of them is aware of what happened and says to the other, 'Get up! Go after the guy who stole our blanket!' The other responds, 'Forget it. When he comes back to take the mattress, let's grab him then.'"

#TIL 414. In June 2019, legendary Beatles drummer Ringo Starr told *The Today Show*'s Al Roker that when he was a kid, he used to say that all people should be shot when they turned sixty. He recounted this story days before his eightieth birthday and admitted he had since changed his mind about it.

#TIL 415. Antonio Salieri did not murder Mozart.

#TIL 416. Octopuses (not *octopi*) have three hearts, blue blood, and eight arms. Each arm can be controlled by the animal independently.

#TIL 417. Contrary to the myth that it never snows in Rome, Italy, the city averages one snowstorm every ten years.

#TIL 418. On the April 10, 1978 episode of *The Merv Griffin Show*, astronaut Gordon Cooper, one of the Mercury Seven, said, "People have seen flying saucers at close hand. And in many cases they have been verified on radar. It is ridiculous for anyone to say that they're all completely unreal."

#TIL 419. One of the most important and groundbreaking elements of Dante Alighieri's *The Divine Comedy* is that it was written in the vernacular—Italian—and not Latin. Latin was more common for literature of the era.

#TIL 420. In 1984, Microsoft founder Bill Gates appeared in a print ad for Radio Shack's Tandy 2000 computer.

#TIL 421. Antonio Vivaldi wrote 500 compositions during his life, 230 of which were for violin.

He died in 1741 and was buried in a pauper's grave.

#TIL 422. According to *National Geographic*, the creation of one pound of ground beef requires 1,799 gallons of water.

#TIL 423. In 1973, rock star Alice Cooper sold a line of mascara called "Whiplash." The ad read, "Liberate your eyes with Alice's own unisex mascara." And, "Whip the one you love—get a tube for your best friend too!"

#TIL 424. In 1982, composer and conductor Leonard Bernstein (*West Side Story*) said that fifteen years after first hearing it, The Beatles' "A Day In The Life" (from the *Sgt. Pepper's Lonely Hearts Club Band* album) "still sustained and rejuvenated me."

#TIL 425.   The Vatican Bank is the only bank in the
world that has menu commands in Latin on
its ATM machines.

#TIL 426.   After President James Garfield was shot
on July 2, 1881, fifteen different doctors
explored the president's wounds with their
bare, unwashed hands, trying to find the
second bullet. The first bullet had caused
a superficial arm injury and was recovered.
The President's doctor, Dr. D.W. Bliss, did
not believe in the radical new theory of the
potential danger of bacteria and germs on
open wounds and antiseptic conditions for
surgery were almost unknown in 1881. As part
of his "treatment," they also fed Garfield
"nutritional enemas," consisting of an egg,
bouillon, milk, whiskey, and opium. Because
the rectum does not have any digestion or
absorption capabilities, it is likely Garfield
also began to suffer from dehydration and

malnutrition after several days of this kind of "care." Garfield died seventy-nine days later.

#TIL 427. It is true that chewing gum is not digestible, but it's not true that swallowed gum remains in your system for seven years. Your body will safely pass it within a few days.

#TIL 428. The most popular pizza topping (other than mozzarella, which is a given) in the United States and Canada is pepperoni. For vegetarians, it's mushrooms.

#TIL 429. According to findings from the *2014 U.S. Religious Landscape Study* conducted by the Pew Research Center, 23 percent of Americans consider themselves religiously unaffiliated. This is up seven points from 16 percent in 2007.

#TIL 430. The most commonly confiscated items at the London City Airport (UK) are snow globes.

Second are jams and spreads and third are toiletries. Number ten on the list are furry handcuffs.

#TIL 431. According to a 2017 survey by the Kellogg Company, only a third (34%) of Americans eat breakfast every day.

#TIL 432. In 2019, it was announced that Robert Ballard, the discoverer of the wreck of the *Titanic*, would lead a National Geographic expedition to find Amelia Earhart's plane. He and his team will use an autonomous, unmanned surface vehicle from the University of New Hampshire called a BEN (Bathymetric Explorer and Navigator). The BEN will have equipment with which it can create 3D topographic and acoustic backscatter maps of the seafloor.

#TIL 433. According to the website similarweb.com, the three most visited websites in the world are, in order, Google, YouTube, and Facebook.

#TIL 434. Famous celebrity atheists include Woody Allen, Jodie Foster, Keira Knightley, Kathy Griffin, Brad Pitt, Daniel Radcliffe, and Morgan Freeman.

#TIL 435. In the 1920, legendary magician and spiritualism debunker Harry Houdini offered $10,000 to anyone who could provide physical evidence of paranormal phenomena that could not be explained scientifically. No one ever collected.

#TIL 436. According to the U.S. Environmental Protection Agency (EPA), approximately 400 billion gallons of water are used in the United States every day.

#TIL 437. According to the company Medical Billing Advocates of America, the typical hospital charge to a patient in 2018 for one 325 mg. acetaminophen tablet was $15.00; a box of tissues, $8.00; a pair of gloves for a physician's use, $53; and to hand a patient their medication, $6.25 each time.

#TIL 438. The most stolen books from U.S. libraries are *The Guinness Book of World Records* and *The Bible*.

#TIL 439. In 1913, Wrigley's Spearmint Gum was sold as an aid for indigestion. The print ad showed an older, grey-haired gentleman decked out in a suit with a vest saying "Wrigley's Spearmint is my protection against indigestion." He also states, "It also assures me of an appetite. By stimulating saliva, it makes me *want* food—then helps *digest* it." The ad also tells readers that "It purifies breath and brightens teeth besides." You were also encouraged (non-grammatically) to "BUY IT BY THE BOX" (yes, in all caps) "of most dealers for 85 cents." (The "of" should be "from.")

#TIL 440. When the fifth President of the United States James Monroe left the White House after his presidency, his political debts were so high he was forced to sell off his slaves and all his property to fend off bankruptcy. Now retired Presidents get a pension. Plus.

#TIL 441. Jack Nicholson's legendary line "You can't handle the truth!" from the movie *A Few Good Men* was ad-libbed by Nicholson during filming. The original line in Aaron Sorkin's script was "You already have the truth."

#TIL 442. According to DatingNews.com, there are approximately 2,500 online dating sites in the United States and around 50 million people have used them, with 62 percent of the users being men.

#TIL 443. Americans buy 600 million pounds of candy each year for Halloween. Ninety million pounds of chocolate are sold during Halloween week alone.

#TIL 444. According to *Men's Journal,* 17 percent of Americans sleep completely "unclothed," and 36 percent of sleepers report sleeping soundly through the night without waking, even once.

#TIL 445. As of May 2019, 305 people have died climbing Mount Everest. This has resulted in Nepal establishing new rules about climbing the fabled peak, including providing proof from prospective climbers that they have at least three years experience in high altitude climbing.

#TIL 446. Many historians believe that the first official United States flag was designed by

Francis Hopkinson, not Betsy Ross. In 1780, Hopkinson wrote a letter to the Board of Admiralty claiming he designed the first flag and requesting compensation in the form of a quarter cask of wine. They never paid.

#TIL 447. Feline research has proven that cats that purr can't roar, and cats that roar can't purr.

#TIL 448. According to the publication the *American Book Review*, the single greatest first line in fiction is "Call me Ishmael." from Herman Melville's 1851 novel *Moby-Dick*.

#TIL 449. If a passenger dies during a plane flight, they're usually put in an unoccupied row. They can't be declared dead until the plane lands.

#TIL 450. Journalist and Shakespeare obsessive Eric Minton did a study of which Shakespeare plays were professionally performed the most, going back to 2011. The winner? *A Midsummer Night's Dream.* The top five are rounded out by numbers two through five: *Romeo and Juliet, Twelfth Night, Hamlet,* and *Taming of the Shrew.* The least performed Shakespeare play during the period was *Henry IV, Parts 1 and 2.*

#TIL 451. Founder of the *Ministry of Fun* James Lovell did the math and came to some astonishing conclusions about Santa Claus. Santa has to make 842 million stops around the world on Christmas Eve, which means his sleigh is capable of traveling at 4.6 million miles per hour. This gives him one millisecond of visiting time per household. And he has to carry 4.4 million tons of presents. But everyone knows Santa is magical, so no problem.

#TIL 452. Bram Stoker based his character of Dracula on the real-world monarch the Prince of Wallachia, also known as Vlad the Impaler.

Vlad was known for impaling his enemies on stakes, thus, his nickname.

#TIL 453. According to *Scientific American*, there are 400 trees for every human on Earth, for a total of over three trillion trees. Twelve thousand years ago, there were twice as many trees on Earth. Mankind cuts down fifteen billion trees a year and plants five billion trees.

#TIL 454. In 1936, a common print ad was for weight *gain* supplements for women. One ad had the model saying, "I have plenty of dates since I've put on 10 pounds," and the copy read, "Skinny? New easy way adds 5 to 15 pounds quick."

#TIL 455. InfoTrends estimates that more than one trillion photographs (that's 1,000,000,000,000 pics) are taken annually.

#TIL 456. Technically, vegetarians should not eat Jell-O or marshmallows if they want to be true vegetarians, since both products contain gelatin, which is a meat by-product. (Gelatin is derived from the collagen inside animals' skin and bones.) Also, vegetarians who want to be true to their vegetarianism should not eat Twinkies. They're made with beef fat.

#TIL 457. According to the flight tracking service FlightAware, at any given moment, there are an average of 9,728 planes in the air around the world, carrying 1,270,406 people.

#TIL 458. In 1933, an art book of prints of the ceiling of The Sistine Chapel was confiscated by the U.S. Postal Service because of the presence of "The Last Judgement" panel, which had naked people in it. The Postal Service was excoriated and ridiculed by both the American people and the press to such an extent that they rescinded the confiscation and cancelled the pending legal prosecution.

#TIL 459. The phrase "You've got another thing coming" is a corruption of the original phrase, "You've got another *think* coming."

#TIL 460. It is believed among *ER* fans that in every episode of the enormously popular medical TV series, someone says or asks for a "rib spreader." This was reportedly an inside joke among the writers, producers, and cast. It is not known if this was confirmed by someone chronicling the mention of the term—the *when* and *where*— in all 331 episodes of the show.

#TIL 461. The word "bowdlerize" came from a man named Thomas Bowdler, M.D. In 1818, at the age of sixty-four, Dr. Bowdler, after concluding that parts of some of Shakespeare's works were too dirty, especially for children, set out to remedy this situation by publishing *The Family Shakespeare*. In that abhorrent volume, Bowdler slaughtered the Bard's work, removing even the slightest hint of the salacious or profane. This outrageous, self-righteous act resulted in his name now being a synonym for editing and censoring literary works. Merriam-Webster defines "bowdlerize" as "to expurgate (something, such as a book) by omitting or modifying parts considered vulgar."

#TIL 462. Kuwait is the largest garbage-producing country on Earth. The country produces 4,603 pounds of waster per capita per year.

#TIL 463. On November 18, 1978, 913 "followers" of Jim Jones committed suicide at his Jonestown, Guyana camp in South America because Jones told them to. They killed themselves by drinking cyanide-laced punch. Parents fed the poison to their children. The punch was

Flavor Aid, although initial reports said it was Kool-Aid. Since then, "drink the Kool-Aid" has become an idiom for blind, unthinking allegiance and obedience.

#TIL 464. The most common body part pierced is the earlobe. Genital piercings for either sex are the most painful.

#TIL 465. Two of the stranger forms of ancient divination were bibliomancy and stolisomancy. For bibliomancy, a person suspected of being a wizard or a sorcerer was weighed. If he weighed less than the church's Bible, he was innocent. For stolisomancy, the way a person dressed him- or herself would determine their innocence or guilt.

#TIL 466. One of the criteria for being committed to a Victorian asylum was holding unusual desires or notions, such as believing you had the ability to predict high tides.

#TIL 467. Foot roasting was one of Tomás de Torquemada's favorite forms of torture during the Spanish Inquisition, and it's exactly what it sounds like: The victim's feet were covered in lard and roasted over a fire for hours.

#TIL 468. According to frozendessertsupplies.com, the three favorite ice cream flavors in America are Vanilla, Chocolate, and Cookies 'n Cream. Number one never changes.

#TIL 469. In 2017, New York's Metropolitan Museum of Art released 375,000 images of artworks from its collection, deeming them "public domain," and putting no restrictions on what people can do with them.

#TIL 470. Estimates vary, but generally, Americans pay between $12 and $15 billion annually in bounced check and overdraft fees.

#TIL 471. On August 10, 1982, the state of Virginia executed Frank J. Coppola by electrocution. The procedure was botched, however. Coppola's head caught fire and it took two jolts of electricity to kill him. The execution chamber also filled with smoke.

#TIL 472. Fresh water will freeze at 32 degrees, but seawater will freeze at 28.4 degrees Fahrenheit. It's because of the salt.

#TIL 473. Lee Harvey Oswald, JFK's purported assassin, was shot once in the abdomen by Jack Ruby as Oswald was being transported by police. Ruby placed the barrel of the gun directly against Oswald's stomach, and the bullet went through Oswald's diaphragm, spleen, right kidney, and stomach and cut off his main intestinal artery, as well as his aorta. Oswald lost consciousness almost immediately and was rushed to Parkland Memorial Hospital by ambulance within minutes. Doctors performed surgery and gave him blood transfusions, but the damage was too great. Oswald died at 1:07 P.M. There is no record of Oswald saying anything before or after Jack Ruby shot him.

#TIL 474. In the HBO TV series *The Sopranos*, New York boss Carmine Lupertazzi finds out that New Jersey boss Tony Soprano wore shorts at a pool party and later told Tony, "A don doesn't wear shorts." This came from a real-life encounter star James Gandolfini had with a real-life wiseguy after the pilot aired. The mob guy approached Gandolfini, told him he'd seen the first episode, and said, "A don doesn't wear shorts."

#TIL 475. Fear of public speaking, fear of heights, and fear of bugs and insects are considered to be the three most common phobias of the modern world.

#TIL 476. We've long been told that no two snowflakes are the same, but there *are* identical snowflakes. There's a caveat, though: snowflakes that *look* identical may not be the *same* at the molecular level. This is because there are an estimated 10 quintillion water molecules in a snowflake (a ten followed by eighteen zeroes) and the ways in which they can combine are as close to infinite as we're going to get.

#TIL 477. In the pre-politically correct era of the late nineteenth, early twentieth century, the bottom three categories for IQ measurement were "Idiot" (<70 IQ); "Imbecile" (70-80 IQ); and "Moron" (80-90 IQ).

#TIL 478. The longest running show in Broadway history is *The Phantom of the Opera*. It has been running continuously at the Majestic Theater in New York since January 26, 1988.

#TIL 479. According to Healthline.com, the ten unhealthiest commercial foods a person can eat (based on calories, carbs, and fat content) are Pop Tarts, Arby's Curly Fries, Popeyes Chicken Tenders, Cinnabon Caramel Pecanbon, Starbucks White Chocolate Mocha Frappuccino, Outback Steak House Bloomin' Onion, Burger King Oreo Shake, Corn Dogs, Dunkin' Donuts Glazed Jelly Stick, and the Dairy Queen Royal Reese's Brownie Blizzard.

#TIL 480. Thomas Jefferson invented the swivel chair and brought the french fry to America.

#TIL 481. The song written and performed by a Beatle that is most often misidentified as a Beatles song is John Lennon's "Imagine." John was a *former* Beatle when he recorded the song.

#TIL 482. Area 51, the top secret flight testing facility, was established in Nevada in 1955. According to U.S. policy, though, it did not exist until 2013, when the government went on record that Area 51 was real. Deadly force is allowed to be used on trespassers.

#TIL 483. The "stupid with a flare gun" who started the fire that burned down the Montreux Casino during a Frank Zappa performance and who was immortalized in Deep Purple's "Smoke on the Water" was a Czech refugee who disappeared.

#TIL 484. The dwarf planet Pluto is smaller than the Earth's moon yet has more water on it than the Earth's oceans combined.

#TIL 485. The first hospice in the United States was the Connecticut Hospice, founded in 1974 and located in Branford, Connecticut. It is still an active facility today.

#TIL 486. Ears and noses never stop growing. It's because they're made from cartilage, which divides more as we age.

#TIL 487. According to carcare.org, the ten most common auto repairs in the United states are oil/oil filter changed, wiper blades replacement, replaced air filter, scheduled maintenance, new tires, battery replacement, brake work, antifreeze added, engine tune-up, and wheels aligned/balanced.

#TIL 488. Apple's 2019 drama *The Morning Show* purportedly cost more to make per episode than HBO's *Game of Thrones*. Why? There are no expensive CGI dragons and battles adding to the budget, as far as we know. It's because of the salaries of the three stars, Jennifer Aniston, Reese Witherspoon, and Steve Carrell. According to *The Hollywood Reporter* and *The Financial Times*, Aniston and Witherspoon are each making $1.2 million per episode.

#TIL 489. In the 1940s and 1950s, the sugar industry and candy manufacturers ran ads showing a smiling mother handing her kid a piece of candy. The headline read, "Kids *need* the energy candy gives."

#TIL 490. Supermarket profit margins range between 1 and 3 percent. They make their money on volume.

#TIL 491. Japanese scientists have "resurrected" cells taken from a wooly mammoth that died 28,000 years ago. (The mammoth's name is Yuka.) The March 2019 issue of the journal

Scientific Reports revealed that Japanese scientists extracted the nuclei from Yuka's cells and implanted them in mice. The cells subsequently showed signs of life.

#TIL 492. In 2012, the Smithsonian Institution reported that in the sixteenth and seventeenth centuries, "many Europeans, including royalty, priests and scientists, routinely ingested remedies containing human bones, blood and fat as medicine for everything from headaches to epilepsy. There were few vocal opponents of the practice, even though cannibalism in the newly explored Americas was reviled as a mark of savagery."

#TIL 493. Stephen Sondheim wrote the song "Send in the Clowns" for his 1973 musical, *A Little Night Music*. It is an odd, complex song which varies in meter between 12/8 and 9/8. In the HBO documentary *Six by Sondheim*, the composer says that it was originally intended to be a throwaway song but it became Sondheim's biggest hit after Frank Sinatra and Judy Collins each recorded it.

#TIL 494. A common cause for cancelling an MRI during the procedure is claustrophobia. Approximately 9 percent of people have some type of claustrophobic anxiety and will insist on being removed from the machine. Open MRIs have allowed many claustrophobic people to have the test anyway.

#TIL 495. According to a study reported in the UK *Daily Mail*, the top five most beloved smells are freshly baked bread, bacon, freshly cut grass, coffee, and cakes baking in the oven. The top five worst odors are garbage pails, drains, body odor, sewage, and vomit.

#TIL 496. There is a "Rolling Stones Rock" on Mars and, yes, it was named for the legendary band. NASA's InSight robotic lander caught the small stone rolling across the Martian landscape and decided to name it as a tribute to Mick and the boys.

#TIL 497. There are no stop signs in Paris, France.

#TIL 498. According to LiveScience.com, the Earth will continue to support life for at least another 1.75 billion years. That is assuming mankind doesn't trigger a nuclear holocaust, and that we don't get hit by another dinosaur-killing caliber asteroid.

#TIL 499. Swedish climate activist Greta Thunberg was sixteen years old when she was named Time magazine's 2019 "Person of the Year." On September 20, 2019, Thunberg inspired 4 million people to strike to call attention to the global climate crisis. According to *Time*, this was "the largest climate demonstration in human history." Did we mention she was sixteen years old?

#TIL 500. The period [.] is the most used punctuation mark in writing, which totally makes sense, because every standard written sentence, even if it has no other punctuation, has to come to an end. And so does this book. Ta-da!

ACKNOWLEDGMENTS

The archetype of the solitary writer toiling away in his or her garret to create their latest epic notwithstanding, writing a book is most assuredly *not* a solo effort. Thus, my gratitude to the following fine folks:

- Thanks and endless love to **Valerie Barnes,** who never gets tired of hearing about the book I happen to be working on. (Or if she does, she hides it very well.)

- Boundless gratitude to my literary agent, the inestimable **John White**, who took on an unpublished author almost forty years ago and has been in my corner ever since, in more ways than I can describe.

- Special thanks to **Mike Lewis**, my partner in literary pandemonium for decades now, and one of the finest examples I know of a generous and kind human being and artist.

- Also, thanks and love to a crew of stalwarts and supporters, without whom . . .

  all my friends at **Laurel Woods**—especially **Amanda, Mary, Nick, Ann Marie**, and both **Steves**—**Janet Daniw, Andy Rausch, Tony** and **Gena Northrup, Dave Hinchberger, Lee Mandato, Rachel Montgomery, Jim Cole**, and anyone who has ever been gracious enough to ask, "So what are you working on?"

- And tremendous thanks and appreciation to my Skyhorse team, including **Michael Campbell**, and my editors **Oren Eades** and **Cory Allyn** for helping to make this book better with every thought, comment, and edit they offered. Also, thanks to **Emily Wood** for her editing skills and meticulous work on this book.

ABOUT THE AUTHOR

STEPHEN SPIGNESI is a writer and author of more than 70 books, and a retired Practitioner-in-Residence from the University of New Haven where he taught composition and literature for ten years. He writes extensively about popular culture and is considered an authority on Stephen King, the Beatles, Elton John, Robin Williams, Woody Allen, *The Sopranos, The Andy Griffith Show, ER*, and other pop culture subjects and TV shows. His other areas of interest and expertise include American history, the US presidents and Founding Founders, the *Titanic*, true crime, and the paranormal. Spignesi was christened "the world's leading authority on Stephen

King" by *Entertainment Weekly* magazine and taught the courses "The New Gothic Horror of Stephen King" and "The Legacy of the *Titanic*" at the University of New Haven. He appears in the A&E *Biography* of Stephen King and the ITV documentary *Autopsy: Robin Williams*. His first novel, *Dialogues* (Random House), was hailed as a "reinvention of the psychological thriller." He lives in New Haven, Connecticut, with his cat Chloe.